WHO IS
MOTHER
GOD?

TONY SCAZZERO

outskirtspress

DENVER, COLORADO

Dedicated to Mother God and Father God

Contents

Preface

For over forty years I have been studying the will of God through the teachings of Sun Myung Moon. My greatest challenge has been observing how life on earth can be hell while knowing God's desire is the Kingdom of Heaven. There is clear disconnection between our reality and God's ideal. How long can this inconsistency continue and how can we reverse this dilemma? When governments spy on their citizens, when the medical establishment hides natural cures, when influential people conspire with secret agendas, when the scientific community fails to conduct metaphysical research, when educational programs do not allow students to think for themselves, or when religious people overlook how to help individuals make a personal relationship with God – it is time to reflect, ask questions, and find better answers.

Through physical and spiritual investigation, it became apparent that there was an almost diabolical cover-up or conspiracy of the highest level – a deliberate disregard for the feminine nature of God. Paradoxically, the Divine Feminine was hidden from view by many traditional religions. In simple terms, Father God has been recognized but Mother God was not. The result has been a huge imbalance because of the one-side way humanity looked toward heaven and the way it reflected back. We currently inhabit a society that ravages the earth, mistreats women and denies deity a female side. The subsequent effects have caused tremendous suffering and disunity all over the world. The treatment can only begin when there is a common appreciation of a gender-balanced, parental Godhead. If the cause is truthful, so will be the result.

The intent of this book is to condense and systematize accessible information so the reader can:

- Examine the early existence of matrifocal cultures centered on the Divine Feminine

- Validate how Mother God is re-emerging through the increased role of women

- Support a balanced masculine/feminine paradigm centered on Mother and Father God.

In earlier times, humankind didn't know about different

sources of energy until they were discovered. Whether it was fire, steam, electric, or nuclear – they were always there until they were discovered. Similarly, Mother God is waiting to be discovered. Just because most people on earth are not aware of her infinite maternal energy does not mean She is not real and present. In fact, the lost of the divine feminine from consciousness is a deficiency we all carry.

Mother God's personal biography is a mystifying story that begins before the dawn of recorded history. For a prolonged time in primitive societies, the female was the dominant character in society. Manifestations of a female deity began long before recorded history, so She is sometimes called the prehistoric Goddess. Evidence of female figurines placed in sacred settings, dates back as far as 25,000 BC. But why were past civilizations and religions based on matriarchy and what caused them to change to patriarchy?

Thanks to recent archaeological, anthropological, historical and linguistic discoveries, previous concepts of divine authority once considered "facts" are now being challenged. The use of Father as the name for God presents the most significant barrier to wide acceptance of Mother God. Only by using both motherly and fatherly language can we understand the full meaning of God as parent. Today, repressed beliefs in a female deity, hidden agendas of past patriarchal influence, and new female divine influence on society are being revealed.

Tony Scazzero
September, 2013

Introduction

What is shocking is how relatively little has been written about the female deities who were worshiped in the most ancient periods of human existence. Even more amazing is that the material available has been almost totally ignored in popular literature and general education. Scholars usually quickly disposed of ideas of the female deity as hardly worth discussing. Yet archaeological evidence seems to prove that Her religion existed and flourished in the Near and Middle East for thousands of years before the arrival of the patriarchal Abraham.[1] Yet if truth be told, the name Goddess and Queen of Heaven are found in many historical documents. The more you research each religion – Protestant, Catholic, Judaic, or the many others – the more you find Mother God there. So much so, in fact that you wonder how man could have kept her hidden.[2] Only through stripping away all the dogmas and penetrating to the feminine core of the ancient vision of life can we attempt to understand who the Divine Mother might be.

Arguing that female divinity and women once held power in religion, raises the question: What happened? The popular image of early human society being dominated by males does not actually hold water. The fact is that tens of thousands of years of human culture were shaped and sustained by communities of creative women who were not only mothers but artists, inventors, scientists, physicians, lawgivers, and shamans. In most traditional religions today, the supreme or only deity is male. But what we are now learning is that in most of our ancient traditions both men and women worshiped a Great Mother, a Great Goddess, who was the mother of both divine daughters and divine sons. At the end of prehistory, a matriarchal age was replaced by the patriarchal world with its archetype of the Great Father with its different symbolism, values, and tendencies. But many of the earliest known stories are of a Great Mother; a female giver and nurturer of life, the Goddess of animals, plants, and humans, water, earth and sky.[3] In fact, the whole of life in prehistoric times was inspired by an ardent faith in the Goddess of nature, the source of creation and harmony.

Whether or not the Mother Goddess was the earliest manifestation of the concept of the deity, her symbolism unquestionably has been the most persistent feature in the archaeological record of the ancient world. From the sculptured Venuses of the Gravetti culture in the

Upper Paleolithic, to the emblems and inscriptions of the cult when it became established in the Fertile Crescent, Western Asia, the Indus Valley, the Aegean, and Crete between the fifth and third millennia BC, female goddesses were everywhere. Moreover, it is now becoming increasingly evident that in its dispersal from southern Russia and western Asia, the female goddess was destined to have a widespread influence and to play a significant role in the subsequent development of the Ancient Near Eastern religions from India to the Mediterranean, from Neolithic times to the Christian era.[4]

In ancient male/female partnership societies, woman and the Goddess were identified with both nature and spirituality; neither woman nor nature was devalued and exploited. This mother of the universe teaches compassion for all living beings and appreciation of the sanctity of the earth itself, because it is the body of the Goddess. There was no need to proclaim the superiority of one over the other, of spirit over nature, of man over woman. Then along comes the aggressive, warlike masculine deity image. The suppression of the feminine principle started and gained steam during Judeo-Christian history. The death blow to Goddess culture was delivered by monotheism in which one male, all-powerful and absolute, ruled both the heavens and the earth.[5]

Humanity in both pre-historic and historic cultures has had a yearning to worship a divine female occasionally along with a divine male. In spite of that, patriarchal religious doctrine has attacked the concept of a divine female and suppressed her worship. But no sooner was goddess worship beaten back than it reappeared with renewed vitality.[6] The mystics understood very clearly that we need both the female and the male aspects of God. The feminine face of God not only reflects the deep-seated beliefs of our ancestors, but is encoded in the bloodlines of humanity and cannot be erased.[7] The feminine face of God is deeply rooted within the core of many religious teachings, so to forget or destroy Mother God would be the same as denying part of ourselves. Still for a number of us today, the concept of God as Mother is difficult to grasp.

Civilized humans have lost something of the cosmic consciousness that belonged to our distant ancestors. Nevertheless, slowly it is coming back. We have to understand how and why these ancient millennia of woman-centric cultures have been buried, ignored, denied, passed off as mythology or of primitive historic origin by Western male historians.[8] Over time, this Great Mother was denounced in the name of a superior Father God, affecting the earth and its inhabitants in detrimental ways. Our very sanity is at stake with the continuing dominance of patriarchy and the denial of the cosmic self, that is, the Goddess within us all and us within Her.[9] Finally, after thousands of years of life-denying patriarchal cultures that have ravaged the earth, She is returning.

An attitude of patriarchy is fundamentally at the root of

a culture that allows women to be beaten and abused. Violence against women, including assault, mutilation, murder, infanticide, rape, and neglect, is one of the most pervasive, yet unrecognized evils in the world. The pervasive evil of patriarchy is given legitimacy by the idea of a primarily male or masculine God. Where male is valued over female, women suffer not only psychological harm but physical abuse and death as male violence toward women continues in crisis proportions all over the world today.[10] Human rights should naturally include women's rights. Indeed, when women rights are fully equal to men, peace on earth will come because everyone will have equal rights.

The return of the Divine Feminine or Mother Goddess has enormous religious, social, and political implications. The recent increased influence of women with the re-emergence of Mother God is more than significantly coincidental. This revisiting of the Divine Mother inspires us to hope that we can heal the deep rift between God and humanity, between men and women and between humanity and nature. Although consistently denied in Western religion, Mother God has the power to change deeply held patriarchal attitudes and beliefs. Most people would agree if there is a God the Father who always was, there was also a Mother God and that the world needs a more maternal side to civilization.[11] The recognition of both Father God and Mother God will help bring worldwide harmony on all levels as both men and women learn to accept themselves and each other more naturally, with the ultimate consequence being a universal movement for equal rights and liberties. Men are now being asked to give up some of their hierarchies of power and dominance and make room for the feminine connectedness as it can manifest in their own lives.

In the past, harbingers and omens have predicted a new spiritual age dawning for humankind where the Divine Feminine would be present intimately in all things and activities. Feminine would be present intimately in all things and activities. In contemporary times, there have been more than a few groups that have attempted to restore the role of the feminine in perceiving divinity. This truth is so immense and paradoxical that it cannot be understood by the rational mind, but only through mystical experience. It is through this intimate awareness of both the masculine and feminine aspect of God that one can fully connect with the divine.

Understanding the meaning of mother is a universal experience yet few of us are familiar and comfortable with talk of God as our Heavenly Mother. We are all like orphans, born in a broken family, because we don't know our divine parents. Even if we don't know who we are, we can call out anywhere at any time to our Divine Mother and experience a real love. Loneliness, suffering and misery can be almost immediately alleviated through conferring with Mother God. Decisions can be properly made on all levels when there is a clear vertical relationship. Once governments, organizations, families and individuals consult with Mother God, all problems can be solved perfectly.

1

The Great Goddess:
Divine Feminine from the Past to the Present

Today the model of a male God dominates the complex makeup of most religions in spite of the fact that since the beginning of *homo sapiens's* existence a female divinity appears to have been greatly honored. Humanity has experienced two types of cultures: the first was in prehistory, when the idea of God as female prevailed; the second was the last few thousand years of recorded history, when God was considered male. Despite massive archaeological evidence, the former is still poorly understood. Ironically, the earlier feminine prehistoric period was more egalitarian, peaceful, and elevated spiritually. Its architecture, geographic distribution, and ornamental graphics reveal a perfectly coherent system of thought and a remarkably enduring notion of a Mother Goddess protecting the living and the dead.[12] In the original religion of the Great Mother, body, mind, and spirit are always integrated. The fact is, women have instinctively guided human evolution, including the spiritual side of life. How and why did this change?

The conflict of the masculine world with the primitive Mother Goddess tradition has been constantly evolving. Yet it is difficult, if not impossible, to get rid of the feminine concept existing since the beginning of time, though the image of the woman only resurfaced by taking on aspects conforming to a new standard. One consequence was the astonishingly prosperous reign of the Virgin Mother of the one, unique God, known by various names and dedications over the course of the centuries.[13] In many cases, the Virgin Mary is in reality, pagan idols put into the service of the Christian religion. Whatever differences there were between them, the Church Fathers did respond to this longing so deeply rooted at the very base of the soul. Although it is difficult to place the various representations in chronological order, they all testify to the permanence of the worship of the Mother Goddess. It is difficult not to admit how striking the parallels are between the Christian Virgin Mary and the Mother Goddess of the third century AD.[14]

By studying what remains of Far Eastern religions, the claim can be made that almost throughout China, in Korea, and Japan, indeed even in eastern Siberia, there was a sun-goddess cult dedicated to Ameteratsu, who, despite her Asiatic overtones, strongly resembles the solar divinities of the West, all originally feminine.[15] In India, the union of Shiva and Parvati is the Great Mother who gives life and nurtures her children. She is also Shakti, that essential female divine energy that is indispensable to any male god who wants to influence the world. Greek legends have tried to explain the transition from feminine cults to masculine ones and mark this reversal of spiritual polarity in different times and places. And in borrowing the Greek's mythology and adapting it to their own mentality, the Romans only facilitated the disintegration of the Great Goddess's primitive image into multiple fantastical constructs.[16]

There is no doubt that, throughout the world, people have felt the need to represent the Goddess with a maternal image, whether it be part of an Earth Mother, a Virgin Mother, or some similar spiritual nature. The very fact that pre-Christian religions worshiped a Mother Goddess made the transition from one ideology to another easy; the ritual remained the same.[17] As one cult representing the divine entity succeeded another, new pilgrimages, legends, and venerations were developed echoing the old. By all evidence, it is because the Magdalene corresponded to a certain image of the Goddess of the beginnings that she was exalted.[18]

In particular, the Virgin Mary would take the place of all the goddesses of antiquity, watering down the traits, giving up their sexuality, but remaining always the one

who gives life and nurtures.[19] The statues that were
constantly displaced, destroyed, then re-supplanted in
sanctuaries were eloquent testimony to the enduring
worship of the Mother Goddess. It seemed impossible
for the memory of the ancient female goddess to be
erased from the popular imagination. From the end
of the nineteenth century until the present, more appearances of the Virgin have been recorded than ever
before. Especially, appearances of Our Lady at Fatima,
Guadalupe, and Lourdes are symbols of a popular fer-
vor deeply rooted in the collective unconscious. Even
if it never openly admits to it, humanity is engaged in
a perpetual quest for the Mother who nourishes her
children, consoles them in their misfortune, and guides
them along the shores leading to the other world.[20]

But no matter how it is expressed, the dominant concept is that of a "mother" of all people. The Virgin is not
only the Mother of God, she is the universal Mother.
Here is the deep meaning of the Christian quest, a message lost but that re-emerges from the human subconscious through the work of artists, clearly inspired by
the Spirit.[21] Most Christian sanctuaries were built on sacred sites known since prehistoric times. The collective
unconscious of the rural population ensured that the
beautiful figure of the divine Mother was maintained,
taking on various tones and complexions according to
the area or the period. All the wooden or stone statues derived from popular art tradition more closely
conform to the deep beliefs buried in the collective

unconscious than to modes imposed by intransigent clergy. And these are all the more significant as they were not imposed by a dominant ideology but emerged naturally from a tradition that was never lost.[22]

2

The Return of the Mother

A celebrated vision of the Divine Mother has always appeared in the mythology of tribal cultures. Only recently has a fresh treasure of insight been discovered from these mythologies of the Divine Mother. We need to bring it back into conscious light in order to learn from it new modes of loving and action that are crucial to our survival. We have silenced many of the gentle feminine voices that could have warned or guided us at the very moment when we most needed their inspiration.[23] The facts of our global crisis, a crisis at once political and economic, psychological and environmental, shows us clearly that the human race has no hope of survival unless it chooses to undergo a total transformation, a total change of heart.[24] Over the last hundred years, greedy and amoral people have cause tremendous damage. Human survival depends on turning to the divine inside of us to learn how we need to go forward. The divination of humanity will release us from the long tyranny of religions into a direct relationship with the Divine Mother. Required of us is an extreme sense of responsibility and adulthood, confronting where we are now and what we need to do and become. If we continue to deny, ignore, and betray the Mother of us all, we will have to face the possible death of everything and everyone we love.[25] When we grow in divine consciousness, there will be no difference between our will and hers, no motive except her impulsion in us, and no action that is not her conscious action in and through us. The moment we start surrendering more and more to the Divine Mother, it will not be us but her doing it through us, in us, as us. This brings tremendous calmness, bliss, and energy.[26]

We are here to become divine human - to have the complete experience of God living in all dimensions simultaneously and spontaneously, savoring all aspects of divine life in one supreme, complete existence. By giving birth to the divine child in ourselves, we realize the innate divinity of our humanness. It is the experience of divine childhood that the Mother now wants to give the human race directly, so we know our humble royalty and the splendor of the world we live in. The world will be saved only by and for the divine children who have awakened in the Mother to the fullness of their and her being, and have become living transmitters of her sacred energy.[27]

The human race began with the Divine Mother, and despite a long tragic journey away from her, must return to her. The Divine Mother wants the human race to embody complete freedom, with the living knowledge of innate divinity. The next stage of human development can unfold through impassioned co-creation and participation in the will, love, and power of the sacred feminine. And in this love of the Mother an entirely new human life will flower in a saved, preserved, beautified, and adored world.[28] The Divine Mother surrounds us at all moments and connects us all together. This wonderful source of feminine enlightenment will bring compassion and true wisdom to this world of suffering. All these are crucial to the Mother revolution, to the revolution of the sacred feminine.[29]

The divine light of the Divine Mother has always been here and the universe is burning in it. Call it to work in any path you take – Christian, Hindu, Taoist, Buddhist, Muslim – any path at all, and the Mother's light will take you with extraordinary intensity, efficiency, and passion to the heart of the transformation you desire. Becoming aware of the miracle of the presence of this light, its availability to everyone everywhere, beyond all theologies and rituals and dogmas, is essential for the survival and transformation of us all. The choice to turn toward it is still and always, ours.[30] Imagine how a world of lovingly independent children would honor and adore each other. They would work to see that the world mirror the beauty and justice of the Divine Mother.[31]

The future of the human race will be made by the Mother and for the Mother by her divine children. Anything that prevents us from attaining this intimate relationship – any dogma, tradition, church, or minister – will have to vanish. Yet it is obvious that the Mother is now shaking the whole earth in a violent set of convulsions designed to bring us to our collective senses, to wake us up inescapably to our responsibilities. We have to know what we have done, but we also have to know that there is an aspect of the godhead that wants nothing more for us than our total transformation and that is streaming toward us at all moments a great, endless flow of unconditional grace. We need an image of the divine that even now, even at this late moment, even after all we have done, offers us compassion, grace, calmness, humor, and passionate and patient encouragement.[32]

3

The Sophia Teachings

The word Sophia refers to a living being who is the Divine Mother of humanity, one who cares for every one of us, who is deeply concerned about what is taking place in the world at the present time, and who is now drawing close to humanity at this time of crisis. Sophia is a being who through immense love for every human being on this planet is concerned with finding a way out of the impasse we face.[33] Throughout history, Sophia, as the mother of humanity, has revealed herself over and over again to different peoples with different traditions and religions. Her presence is ever-present in the major spiritual traditions of the world.

Sophia has been the shaping influence of major transitions in human culture and evolution. She has not only been the inspiration for Solomon's temple but also the inspiration of philosophy in Greece. Through her divine wisdom human beings could begin to form a new relationship with her through the use of the power of thought. This is what gave birth to philosophy. When we consider the original meaning of the word philosophy, *philosophia*, or love of Sophia, we can see it was really love for the Divine Sophia, who was present from the very beginning as the divine plan of creation that gave birth to philosophy.[34]

The teachings of Sophia have a close parallel in other spiritual traditions. In Taoism the Tao is the Divine Mother, the mother of all things. The aspect of the Divine Feminine in Hinduism is Kali, a consort of Shiva. Also Radha, the consort of Krishna, is one of the central deities of the Hindu religion. Also in Hinduism, the Divine Mother manifests herself as Nature or Mother Earth. In Buddhism, Prajna corresponds to the Hindu Shakti or Divine Mother. Prajna manifests in Buddhism as the goddess Tara. In Chinese Buddhism, Kuan Yin is the goddess of mercy. Within the Christian tradition, millions of people have been touched in some way and healed by Sophia incarnated within the Virgin Mary, with many apparitions taking place around the world.[35]

Today we are at the moment of a paradigm change when the Divine Feminine, Sophia, the Holy Spirit will usher in a new age. Her gifts, especially those of love and compassion, will become more prominent and evident among all people as She becomes more visibly present in each one of us. Living in and with Her gifts of divine love, we slowly will transform this world into the Kingdom of God.[36] Sophia is calling women to leave behind the masculine spirituality that is all around them and adopt a spirituality that speaks to their spirit and soul, a spirituality that they can feel and sense, one that will lead them deeper into their femininity.

Science and technology have now reached a point of crisis, and a new direction has to emerge. There has been a one-sided masculine direction of development, and there needs to be a reorientation to the divine wisdom of Sophia. The gradual disappearance of Sophia in the West, causing her to be lost or concealed, has diminished humanity's creative power of thinking. The feeling of the Divine Feminine and the relationship to the Divine Sophia was lost in Christianity. As a result, the whole evolution of Christianity has been in the spirit of a one-sided rational development that parallels the development of modern science and technology. The feminine mode of thought, the thinking of the heart, became more and more excluded from Christian thinking, and now this imbalance needs to be corrected.[37] The challenge of our time is to welcome Divine Sophia into our lives and to let divine wisdom begin to speak to us again. We need to allow this wisdom, which has been held back for so long, to become the inspiring, guiding voice in human hearts now and in the future.

It is Sophia's hope, as the mother of humanity, that her children will find a new relationship to her and will enter into connection with her in a new and creative way. Divine Sophia can speak to us in a new way, in her ageless wisdom, as the comforter and caring mother of humanity. In our modern times her guiding influence will redress the imbalance caused by one-sided rational and scientific development, and offer the possibility of bringing the Divine Masculine and Feminine into balance within each human being. The great promise is that, with our cooperation, Divine Sophia will be the guiding power and inspiration for the next transition in humanity's evolution.[38]

Sophia is a divine being who can speak to us of the mystery of existence, of the wonder and glory of God's creation, and of all that radiates from every aspect of the creation. It is Sophia who opens up to us the mysteries of the seasons, of the relationships between earth and the cosmos, the healing properties of plants, and the mysteries of the animal kingdom and the true relationship between humanity and the animal, plant, and mineral kingdoms. It is Sophia who reveals to us the properties of the different precious stones and their healing powers.[39] The temple of Solomon was a unique and majestic work, a manifestation of the divine and a testimony to divine inspiration. Solomon received wisdom and understanding from Sophia on how to build the temple when he turned to her in prayer. Sophia reveals herself to any human being who upholds the path of justice and righteousness. Martin Luther King Jr. and Mahatma Gandhi are good examples. From age to age, Sophia enters into holy souls and all those who seek her.[40]

Now is the time to renew our connection to the Divine Feminine. A turning point in a spiritual evolution is coming that will signify the beginning of a transformation and spiritualization of the whole earth. The creation of a new Heaven and a new Earth signifies the awakening to the Divine Mother and an awakening to Sophia as the World Soul. More and more human beings will begin to find a paradisiacal quality in our relation to nature and will begin to experience a new connection and unity with the entire planet. Understanding the message of the Sophia teachings is essential for a true grasp of the start of the New Age, and it's unfolding during the new millennium.[41]

If we look at our present world, we see how impoverished we are through failing to turn to the Divine Feminine. It is important, even crucial, that the Divine Feminine become a new power of inspiration in human affairs. Sophia has the possibility of becoming the shaping influence for civilization as the future unfolds. We are now entering a new era, one in which Sophia is attempting to become more and more part of our lives as a guide and inspiration. And for every problem that we have in our lives, every question of destiny, we can turn to Sophia as a source of guidance, help, and inner strength.[42]

4

The Return of the Feminine

The world has been terribly damaged and needs to be healed. The tragic imbalance of the masculine has brought humankind to the point of disaster, and unless we recover the feminine powers of the psyche, life on the planet will never progress. Men can't heal the world, especially as they are the cause of the ecological and spiritual desecration that has happened. Women are needed in this healing because women have the magical substance in their being that has to do with the real mystery of creation. One of the first steps is that women have to forgive the masculine, or men, for what they have done. No healing can be happen without forgiveness. After that, what happens is very mysterious. A higher energy comes down through a woman's spiritual body, then through her physical body into the world to heal it.

Only the spiritual work of women can accomplish this undertaking.

The sacred wholeness of life belongs to the feminine aspect of the divine, the Great Goddess. For Her, every act is sacred; every blade of grass, every creature is a part of the Great Oneness. Along with Her awe-inspiring transcendence, She embodies the caring divine presence. The Native American, among other tribal cultures, honored this aspect of the Great Mother. Reinstating the Goddess means restoring the sacredness of a nurturing, all-embracing divinity. God's masculine omnipotence and transcendence need to be balanced by the feminine aspects of care and nearness.[43]

The days of the priestesses, with their temples and ceremonies, are over, and because the wisdom of the feminine was not written down but transmitted orally, this sacred knowledge was lost. We cannot reclaim the past, but we can witness a world without Her presence, a world that we exploit for greed and power, that we rape and pollute without real concern. And then we can begin the work of welcoming Her back, of reconnecting with the divine that is at the core of creation and learning once again how to work with the sacred principles of life. Without the intercession of the Divine Feminine we will remain in this physical and spiritual wasteland we have created, passing on to our children a diseased and desecrated world.[44]

The mystery of the Divine Feminine speaks to us from within Her creation. She is not a distant god in heaven but a presence here with us, needing our response. She is the divine returning to claim Her creation, the real wonder of what it means to be alive. We have forgotten Her, just was we have forgotten so much of what is sacred, and yet She is always part of us. But She now needs to be known again, not just as a myth, as a spiritual image, but as something that belongs to the blood and the breath. She can help us to give birth to the divine that is within us, to the oneness that is all around us. She can help us remember our real nature.[45]

To fully encounter the Divine Feminine, the creative principle of life, we must be fully prepared for Her anger at the pain that has come from Her abuse. For centuries our masculine culture has repressed Her natural power, has burnt Her temples, killed Her priestesses. Through his drive for mastery, and his fear of the feminine, of what he cannot understand or control, the patriarchy has not just neglected Her, but deliberately tortured and destroyed Her. He has not just raped Her but torn the very fabric of life, the primal wholeness of which She is always the guardian. And the feminine is angry, even if Her anger has been repressed along with Her magic.[46]

Now it is time for the wisdom of the feminine to be combined with masculine consciousness, so that a new understanding of the wholeness of life can be used to heal our world. Our present scientific solutions come from the masculine tools of analysis, the very mind-set of separation that has caused the problems. We cannot afford to isolate ourselves from the whole anymore, and the fact that our problems are global illustrates this. By combining masculine and feminine wisdom, we can come to understand the relationships between the parts and the whole, and as we listen we can hear life telling us how to redress this imbalance.[47]

Mother God is going to tell us what to do because She has been around a lot longer than we have. We have forgotten about Her for so long, but She is alive. She is here now. And She is waiting for us to respond. She needs the participation of all who are open to this work. The work of the feminine is how to reconnect with Her and live Her sacred knowing, despite the real fears of being attacked. Then the feminine will teach us how to live life and reveal its secret meanings.

We need the magical powers within nature to heal and transform this world. But awakening these powers would mean that our patriarchal institutions would lose their control, as once again the mysterious inner world will come into play, releasing forces once understood and used by the priestess and the shaman, whose existence the patriarchal world has forgotten. The science of the future will work with these forces, exploring how the different worlds interrelate, including how the energies of the inner can be used in the outer. The shaman and the scientist will work together as the wisdom of the priestess and the wisdom of the physician renew their ancient connection.[48]

Without the participation of the Divine Feminine, nothing new can be born. The feminine can give us an understanding of how all the diverse parts of life relate together, their patterns of relationship, the interconnections that nourish life. She can help us see consciously what She knows instinctively: that all is part of a living, organic whole, in which all parts of creation express the whole in a unique way. An understanding of the organic wholeness of life belongs to the instinctual knowing of the feminine, but combined with masculine consciousness this can be communicated in words, not just feelings. We can be given a blueprint of the planet that will enable us to live in creative harmony with all of life.[49]

Through the light of the direct feminine knowing, life can quickly reconnect with its own divine nature, and the divine can transform life in ways that we cannot imagine. With our ordinary consciousness we cannot heal and transform the world of the effects of our pollution – it would take too long to redeem what we have destroyed. But the presence of the divine can awaken the world to its magical and miraculous power. If we welcome the divine back into life, if we acknowledge her divine nature – than we can participate in life's re-creation, in the miracle that is waiting to happen.[50]

5

Rebirth of the Goddess

In the classical mythology of Greece, each of the goddesses is deprived of power that once was hers. These goddesses, including Athena, Aphrodite, Artemis, Inanna, and Ishtar come from the warrior societies of the Bronze and Iron Ages. These ancient goddess cultures were woman-centered, nonviolent, and progressive. In spite of this, in the mythologies of these cultures the goddesses of the Neolithic and Paleolithic eras are slain or made subordinate to the new gods of the patriarchal warriors, such as Zeus and Marduk. Their goal is to dethrone the goddess and to legitimate the new culture of the patriarchal warriors. Subsequently, the Divine Feminine has suffered and had her history stolen from her, and this has affected all of us.[51]

There were many primitive goddesses known throughout the world. Each one is said to have had different capabilities and a different name. Artemis was the hunt-ing goddess of the Greeks. Sedna and Chukchi were goddesses that provided the Eskimos with food. The great goddess of the Siouan tribes of North America, First Woman was also the mother of vegetable and animal food. The great goddesses of Western Asia are Earth Mothers who bring forth the corn. Primitive ag-ricultural goddesses retain the character of the primitive universal mother, the mother of God.[52] The point may be illustrated from Mexico, where the Great Mother fulfills the many functions commonly assigned to lunar deities – she was the goddess of all waters, the source of diseases and of healing, and the protectress of women and of child bearing. The great goddesses owed their existence not to the earth but to their motherhood.[53]

Women had an important influence in the evolution of religion and religious ideas. The fierce tribal gods of hunters became transformed under the influence of the women's religion, their attributes changing in harmony with the character of the universal Mother. The Great Mother and the divine child were the first divinities to whom women, at any rate, turned their feeling other than those of dread. Tenderness, love, maternal instincts entered the sphere of religion for the first time. Hitherto, all spirits, tribal gods, sky gods, had been feared and pla-cated. Later when the heavenly fathers who had almost faded out of existence reasserted themselves, the Queen of Heaven was put away by a solitary God.[54]

The most striking feature of the earliest Aegean civilization, centered on Crete, is the predominance of female deities. No male idols have been found, yet the
goddess's primitive character was preserved, above all,
by her relation to the male gods with whom she was associated. These gods are not her husbands or consorts,
but complementary matching parts. Divine pairs are
merely male and female aspects of the same divinity.
Such pairs were the general rule in primitive Semitic religion and are found in native Italian cults. Sometimes
these pairs are sharply contrasted as masculine and
feminine principles – as heaven and earth.[55]

At any rate, the Goddess and Mother roles within modern
culture seem to be reemerging. While the psychoanalyst
Sigmund Freud down-played the emergence of devotion to the Goddess as an infantile desire to be reunited
with the mother, his theory was challenged by C.J. Jung,
who described this emergent devotion as "a potent force
of the unconscious." Jung theorized that "the feminine
principle as a universal archetype, a primordial, instinctual pattern of behavior deeply imprinted on the human
psyche, brought the Goddess once more into popular
imagination." The anima and animus are described by
Jung as elements of his theory of the collective unconscious, a domain of the unconscious that transcends the
personal psyche. In the unconscious of the male, this archetype finds expression as a feminine inner personality:
anima; equivalently, in the unconscious of the female it
is expressed as a masculine inner personality: animus.

A number of men have expressed the need to return to the Goddess, indicating that this is not only a woman's search or desire. Some renowned authorities believe that every man in Western culture also needs this vital connection to the vital female principle in nature and urge men to turn to the Goddess. There are various views on the causes, but "Jungians have espoused the Mother Goddess as an archetype, a loadstone in the collective consciousness of both men and women to be minded of psychological wholeness." In this way men will be able to relate to women on more equal terms, not fearful or resentful of female power. Possibly this is how it was in prehistoric times when men and women coexisted peacefully under the hegemony of the Goddess.

Although it is increasingly recognized that a new religion of the Goddess is being created, some resist it. The process of discovering and experiencing connections with the Goddess as Mother God is both intelligent and intuitive. The Goddess is a powerfully transformative metaphor that can break the hold of male control that has shaped our images not only of God but of all the significant power in the universe. Conventional theology has all too often told us what to think, stifled questions, and denied personal experiences. The Goddess who manifests in our lives today speaks our language and suggests courses of action suitable to our times. The Goddess experience and rituals challenge the pervasive dualism of Western culture while at the same time they connect us to a divinity who is known within nature and who personifies change.[56]

6

The Goddess Religion

Most people become flustered, upset, and even angry when it is suggested that the God they know as Lord and Father might also be called God the Mother or Goddess. Images of the Goddess help to break the hold of male control that has shaped our images not only of God but of all significant power in the universe. This new insight may come in a flash but it may also take years of living with images of the Goddess, both verbal and visual, before it settles fully into the consciousness. Eventually, personal experiences, especially communal ones, confirm the Goddess' reality.

Goddess religion challenges theologians and historians of religion to reformulate foundational theories of divinity and the origins of religion. Mother God is both the one we had not known and the one we had always known. As a result, knowing that the world was once different than it is now can be a source of enormous hope as well as great despair. A society that reveres nature and the feminine creates beauty, love, and equality. The symbols and rituals of Goddess religion bring these values to consciousness and help us build communities in which we can create a more just, peaceful, and harmonious world.

In a true Goddess religion, Mother God is fully within the world and within us. She is both immanent and transcendent. Mother God is internally related to everything in the world. This means she is affected in the depth of Her being by everything that exists and everything that happens in the world. She resonates with both our joy and in our suffering. As fully embodied in and related to the world, Her power is limited both by the laws of nature and the weight of history. Mother God cannot control the universal principles that guide the laws of nature. She is also affected both positively and negatively by the events that occur in the world. When the world is suffering, She is diminished; when the world is joyous, She is enhanced.[57]

As fully immanent, the Goddess is embodied in the finite, changing world. She is known in the rock and the flower and in the human heart. As the organism uniting the cells of the earth body, the Goddess is the firm foundation of changing life. As the mind, soul, or enlivening power of the world body, the Goddess is intelligent, aware, alive, a kind of "person" with whom we can enter into a relationship. Thus the Goddess can speak to us through the natural world, through human relationships, through communities, and through dreams or visions, expressing her desire to manifest life ever more fully in the world. And we can "speak" to her in song, meditation, prayer, and ritual, manifesting our desire to attune ourselves with her rhythms, to experience our union with the body of the earth and all beings who live upon it.[58]

The Goddess seeks the greatest good for the greatest number of beings, but her power is limited. The Goddess cannot change the natural cycles of birth, death and renewal that form the context of all life because the Goddess does not stand outside the laws of nature. The cycles of nature are her cycles. Death is not the enemy. It is part of the circle of life. The relation of the Goddess to the history of species and to human history is more complex. Here, her power is persuasive but not coercive.[59] Goddess power attempts to inspire all beings to respect life and to seek harmony and balance. Everything that happens is the world is not the will of the Goddess, because each person has free will.

The Goddess is always attempting to persuade us to love intelligently, concretely, and inclusively. When we do so, she rejoices. But the Goddess can influence and inspire us only if we open ourselves to her power. She must work in and through finite individuals who may resist her power and within communities with jaded

histories. When we violate the web of life, we fail to recognize or deny the persuasions of the Goddess. Because
her power is not coercive, the Goddess depends on us,
as we depend on her. But her power is real and our
power becomes greater when we work in conjunction
with her.[60] The power of the Goddess is a limited power that operates within a finite and changeable world.
She cannot transform the crises that the world faces –
historical injustice, environmental destruction and pollution, the threat of nuclear catastrophe – without the
cooperation of all those who affect it.

Will the Goddess religion be unfair to men as God religion has been to women? We must remember that the
Goddess is emerging at a time when women, women's
bodies, and nature have been devalued and violated for
centuries. In this context, the metaphor of the Goddess
has the power to shatter long-standing cultural attitudes and prejudices about women and nature. The
Goddess as metaphor brings healing to our historical
situation. And while it is true that the Goddess is a
powerful symbol for women, increasing numbers of
men are recognizing her power to bring healing to their
lives also.

The principles and ethics of the Goddess religion
include:[61]

- Nurture life

- Walk in love and beauty

- Trust the knowledge that comes through the body

- Speak the truth about conflict, pain, and suffering

- Take only what you need

- Think about the consequences of your actions for seven generations

- Approach the taking of life with great restraint

- Practice great generosity

- Repair the web of life

The Goddess hypothesis challenges historians of religion to abandon their almost exclusive commitment to text, requiring them to accept physical evidence - paintings, sculptures, bones, pots, weavings, etc., as reliable evidence upon which to build new theory. The Goddess hypothesis also challenges biblical and traditional ideas about the nature of God.[62] Once the commitment to text as the only valid form of evidence is broken, historians will be able to come to a clearer understanding of the role of the Paleolithic and Neolithic periods in the shaping of religious history. Ancient images of the goddesses and echoes of their power in later myths and customs challenge current beliefs. As we learn about ancient Goddess religions and cultures, we begin to understand that we do not have to live in a culture that worships one male God, where the domination and control of women, earth, and other people are taken for granted and warfare is perpetual.[63]

Reviewing the past with an open mind will help bridge the gap between the older matriarchal and the newer patriarchal religions. As religious symbols are both models of divine reality and a model for human behavior, they set the tone of culture, suggesting how things should be. Rediscovering new symbols for Mother God can guide humanity's future in a positive direction. By combining the constructive aspects of patriarchal religions with the ethics of the Goddess religion, a beautifully balanced world organism can guide the world back to peace.

7

Gnostic Ideas

There are some obvious inconsistencies between theory and practice in churches today. For instance, in theory most modern Christians would agree we do not imagine God as a bearded patriarch sitting on a throne somewhere up in heaven. Yet in practice, the language of our hymns and prayers and creeds does suggest that we still have this one-sided male image in mind. Within the real experience of Christians across the ages there has always been a powerful egalitarian principle at work against the dominance of the male. What could be more inconsistent than to know in our hearts that men and women are truly equal and then go ahead and speak of God as though the Supreme Being were a male? Thinking about God in different ways could create a paradigm shift that would lead to a more equitable world. It's fundamentally a matter of reflecting and clarifying our faith from the broad range of human experience. But unless the world's great faith traditions begin to affirm an image of God that truly mirrors our own nature, solutions to our gravest problems may not occur.

Even though Christians, Jews and Muslims have devoted two thousand or more years to God the Father, the world still does not resemble heaven on earth. All the troubles in the world indicate that God the Father is also in trouble, so maybe it's time to consider the alternatives. New policy statements from Rome, new peace initiatives from political leaders, and new cultural norms do not seem to be sufficient to address, let alone solve, the problems that confront the world today. Our customary religions and governments seem stifled if not helpless to solve all the enormous challenges that confront us. Political conflicts, social problems, crime, and corruption indicate that perhaps it's time to re-evaluate the current systems in place. To make essential changes to rectify the problems in the world, there has to be a change of heart.

For as long as most of us can remember, we've been taught, by the very people who brought us sex scandals and warfare without end, that the God in whose name such things were perpetrated is an all-powerful Father God. Could it be that there's something in this image of God that actually contributes to the problem and prevents us from finding the solutions we so desperately need? Maybe it is time we take into consideration the female, mothering aspect of God's nature. What better way to emphasize the intimacy of our relationship with God than to imagine a mother's love for her child? When you think of the devotion, the sacrifice, the tenderness, and sometimes the suffering that a mother pours out for her children, doesn't that reflect in some deep way the love God feels for each of us?

Most Christian sects have thought of God as just masculine. Yet there have been a few, like the Gnostics, open-minded enough to follow their instincts and conscience. Their understanding of God included that of a Great Mother, creator and life-giver to all of nature and to everyone in it. Achieving gnosis involves coming to recognize the true source of divine power. Those who come to know that source simultaneously come to know themselves and subsequently discover their spiritual origin: they come to know their true Father and Mother.[64] One group of gnosis sources claims to have received a secret tradition from Jesus through James and Mary Magdalene. Members of this group prayed to both the divine Father and Mother. Gnostic Christians describe God in both masculine and feminine terms with a complementary description of human nature. The Gnostic description of God – as Father, Mother, and Son – may startle us at first, but on reflection, we can recognize it as another version of the trinity.[65]

The Gnostics did not adhere to the orthodox Christian

creed of "I believe in one God Father Almighty, Maker of heaven and earth." They kept the feminine meaning of the Holy Spirit, which remained in their sacred writings and interpretations. In New Testament times, within the early Christian Church there was a strong emphasis upon the maternal aspects of God. Recent archaeological discoveries suggest that many early Christians thought of God as a Being who possessed both masculine and feminine qualities. One group of ancient texts contains prayers addressed to both a Father and a Mother God.

In ancient religions the idea of Mother God was very closely related to the idea of Mother Earth or Mother Nature. In medieval times, language about God was grounded in the life of women as well as men. In this male-dominated, warrior society, people were exposed to a vision of God as Father, lord, and king as well as a nurturing, tender mother, maiden, and midwife. Even in the period of the church's greatest worldly power, there were many who continued to feel God's love and to see in God's love a maternal dimension. It seemed only natural and obvious that a God who gave birth to the world must have at least something in common with a woman who gives birth. As a human mother gave birth to us all, God was quite naturally seen as the Mother of us all.

8

Myth and Reality

At this miserable point of cultural development that has led us into the deadlock of scientific materialism, technological destructiveness, religious nihilism and spiritual impoverishment, a most astounding phenomenon has occurred. An old myth is arising in our midst and asks to be integrated into our modern frame of reference. It is the myth of the ancient Goddess who once ruled earth and heaven before the advent of patriarchy and of patriarchal religions.

While old values are breaking down, a new consciousness is also being born. We seek new forms of self-validation out of relating to our emotional and instinctual urges. Yet, paradoxically these new ways require retrieval of old, seemingly discarded and repressed modes of functioning. The magical, mythological, and feminine ways of dealing with existence, left behind thousands of years ago, must now be reclaimed by our consciousness. But compared to the past, this new consciousness will have to be endowed with greater clarity, freedom, self-awareness, and a new and different capacity to love.[66]

Amidst tremendous transition and upheaval, traditional male and female roles in society are being challenged. The feminine call for new recognition arises simultaneously with the violence that threatens to get out of hand. This strange coincidence eludes our rational understanding. Apparently, our spiritual life cycle again needs divine monitoring. People the world over are wondering why cataclysmic events are happening. One explanation is that it is preparation for a new age. Another is that the ancient Goddess is arising from the depths of the unconscious psyche. If we refuse to acknowledge her, she may unleash forces of destruction. If we grant the Goddess her due, she may compassionately guide us toward transformation.[67]

Honoring not only God but the Goddess is a life-changing, world-renewing tradition that goes beyond time and space. It calls for service to the earth and the community and is a radical way to confront injustice, corruption, and any imbalance in the system. Amazingly the Goddess religion is unimaginably old but contemporary.[68] The return of the Great Goddess is necessary to help adjust our thinking to overcome the problems of life. She stresses the feminine, earthly, instinctual, and sensitive aspects of existence. These changes entail new understandings of masculinity and femininity in both men and women and the relations between the sexes, as well as new views of reality. The estrangement from nature and from ourselves is caused by a warped and unrealistic view of reality. The estrangement from nature and from ourselves is caused by a warped and unrealistic view of reality. Incredibly, this abnormal view of reality is caused by believing in myths.

There are four great myths that are causing increasing alienation from the maternal cosmic organism: the divine kingship, the human exile of loss paradise, the propitiatory sacrifice of the scapegoat, and the inferiority of the feminine. Unbeknownst to us, these myths still underlie to a large extent our modern world-view. Since we no longer think and feel mythologically in a conscious way, we now rationalize them. They have become unconscious fantasy premises and illusions that seem real. They determine our conscious ethos, our social values, and our modern religion, which now goes under the name of science.[69]

With the present state of technological development, uncurbed violence many mean the disintegration of social structure, nuclear holocaust, and collective suicide. Yet we have no satisfactory cure for this threat. Attempts to regulate violent aggression or, for that matter, greed by law, Christian charity, ethical principles, social reform, and good will are no longer adequate.

We need religious-cultural systems capable of defusing aggression, anger, and violence and directing them into constructive channels. Yet we have none. Our traditional patriarchal religions no longer help us to contain them. Often, therefore, we are naively unprepared for each new trauma or assault. We are shocked, or worse, we are not even shocked because we expect it.[70]

The only remedy left is to overcome our resentment toward the feminine and embrace her.

9

Mother God

For many centuries, history gave almost all the credit to the Heavenly Father. There is a blatant imbalance rooted in the Father-son relationship while ignoring the presence of the feminine aspect of the love of God. Men build their strength on the foundation of God being masculine. We should understand that it was not only Father God who carried human history. Just because it is convenient to use the pronoun He and awkward to use the pronoun She, does that mean by implication that She had no part in the healing of humankind. In the quantity of human experiences as rated by percentiles, there should be some minimum amount of credit offered to Mother God. Without it, where is Her triumph? Human history has treated God as if She were not a mother. It is equally true that both Father and Mother God want to see their children happy and fulfilled. Leave Mother God out and God becomes a single parent struggling to support everyone. If we recognize God, we can understand that God wants to give in superb feminine ways as well.

People deny the mothering aspect of God because throughout history, there were few recorded experiences of communications from God to women, or from women to God. There isn't a lot of examples about having faith in Mother God, in the feminine. The efforts and achievements of the Providence were often too male-centered, ignoring the contributions of Mother God. Today we should understand that God gave of Herself, and She continues to do so. In the past, God's dispensation did not recognize the value of women or even see women and men working together for the benefit of the family.

Mother God is asking us to liberate our minds from narrow conceptions of what it means to relate with God, beyond the scriptures and restrictions of traditional religion. Human beings have to break past habits and come to terms with the true identity of God. She requests that we expand the scope of our communication with God to include all the diverse activities and issues in the lives of women and men, for nothing is off-limits to Mother God. Finally, we can have humanity correctly referring to God in terms of His/Her parental responsibility as Heavenly Parent.

One of the reasons women have been so attracted to Father God is that they see in Him an ultimate example for masculinity, a gauge. Nonetheless, just as humanity has recognized God as having masculine value, it needs to recognize Her feminine value. The feminine concept needs to be awakened in everybody. We need an age for women, because women deserve to receive absolute love, to have a way to attain it, maintain it, and to liaise with God, without fear. They have to learn a new tradition of trusting, even unconditionally, a Divine Mother. Mother God is really what the new age of women is all about.

St. Hildegard was among the first to share her profound vision concerning the femininity of God:

> She watches over all people and all things in heaven and on earth, being of such radiance and brightness that, for the measureless splendor that shines in her, you cannot gaze on her face or the garment she wears. For she is awesome in terror and the Thunderer's lightening, and gentle in goodness as the sunshine. Hence, in her terror and her gentleness, she is incomprehensible to mortals, because of the dread radiance of divinity in her face and the brightness that dwells in her as the robe of her beauty. She is like the sun, which none can contemplate in its blazing face or in the glorious garment of its rays. For She is with all and in all, and of beauty so great in her mystery that no one could

know how sweetly she bears with people, and what unfathomable mercy she spares them.[71]

Many groups did not want it to be let out that there was a Mother God because they were afraid they would be called heretics or ignorant.[72] Many religions thought that by keeping people in darkness and ignorance, they could maintain control. Patriarchal religions have held people under their thumb, thinking people were too stupid to encompass any larger aspects. Individuals of dogmatic convictions have always had a problem with the Mother Goddess concept because it has belonged to the nature religions, who always believed in Her.

Many spiritual traditions believe there have always been a Mother God and a Father God. Mother and Father God are melded together as a dual entity. They are the other half of each other or the original soul mates. Everyone is imbued with aspects of Mother and Father God.[73] Fundamentally men represent Father God and women represent Mother God. Mother God is a being of pure emotion, the Primary Motivator of life and is the Great Interceptor.[74] She is a dynamic force, full of fire and fury, knowing all the emotions while Father God provides the inspiration, power and straightforward influence.

Every religion has a yin and a yang. Duality exists in all the creation. Every man and woman has both masculine and feminine qualities. The most ancient beliefs were that the female goddess was primary, but this did not diminish males. This is the original mother and father ideology that has gone astray. Father God rules the spiritual world and Mother God rules physical life and everything that has to do with humans and human emotion. She can intercept and make better, alleviate sorrow, and lessen pain. If there are any miracles to be wrought, She is the one who will do it. It is the time of the intercession of the Mother Goddess.[75]

10

The Divine Feminine

Remarkably, many biblical passages depict God in the image of the maternal deity. Not only is the Creator depicted as carrying in the womb or birthing the creation, but also Christ and the Holy Spirit are depicted in similar roles. Many biblical images picture God as the one who carries, feeds, protects, heals, guides, disciplines, comforts, washes, and clothes her human children.[76] The act of wiping away tears from the eyes (Rev.21:4) is traditionally feminine. Isaiah 66:13-14 makes explicit the fact that such comforting often indicates the presence of God's maternal aspect. In Galatians 5:22, Christians are urged to give birth to the fruit or offspring of the Holy Spirit. The point of reclaiming the female component in the supposed masculine God of the Bible is rather to affirm both the masculine and feminine components in every human being and to honor the work that women have done though the centuries alongside the achievements of men.[77]

Orthodox Christian writers have utilized female God images quite often. In the second century, Clement of Alexandria focused on a maternal suckling God. To Clement, the aspect of God's nature that has sympathy with humankind is mother. St. John Chrysostom used allusions to God's motherhood, while Saint Ambrose spoke of the Father's womb and even the nourishing breasts of Christ. Valentius, St, Gregory, St. Augustine, the Venerable Vede, Peter Lombard, St. Thomas Aquinas, and St. Bonaventure were among others who utilized and referred to the divine as mother.[78] Many Cistercian monks tended to use explicit and elaborate maternal imagery to describe God and Christ. Christian women sharing in the tradition of a female, maternal God included Blessed Angela, St. Catherine, St. Bridget, Margery Kemp, Dame Julian, and St. Theresa. By utilizing imagery of God as female, they were simply following the usage of Scripture and the guidance of their own inner experience. Descriptions of God as a woman nursing the soul at her breast, drying its tears, giving birth to it in agony and travail, are part of twelfth-century monastic writing, which spoke of the divine in homey images to emphasize its approachability.[79]

Exclusively male images of God are killing our spirit by distorting our understanding of masculinity and femininity. The recognition of biblical images of God as female, the infusion of positive female images into the language of faith, the achievement of balance between male and female references will do a lot to bring renewed health to spirituality. Studying God images associated with discipline, authority, and tenderness creates a more accurate female image. Reclaiming the biblical images of God as female will help break stereotypes of how a woman ought to behave. More important, from the standpoint of both good literary interpretation and good theology, it is best to follow the overall usage of Scripture, which is to attribute both male and female characteristics to the divine One.[80]

Inclusive God-language is a step in the right direction. Whereas many religious leaders lament their inability to do more to alleviate world hunger, the nuclear threat, and other economic and racial inequalities, their own language is something they could control almost immediately. By recognizing the female presence in their grammatical choices, and by utilizing biblical references to God as female, they could demonstrate the sincerity of their commitment to human justice, peace, and love and therefore to psychological and social health.[81] The image of God as the One Mother of us all should be the main thrust for peace within man's souls and for peace on earth. The entire human race, people of all colors, religions, political and economic systems, are living, moving, and existing within the cosmic womb of the One God.[82]

The male God imagery in the Bible has been implying all along that men are Godlike, and thus empowering men to take total responsibility for society. Stating that women are Godlike is not an attempt to outdo men, but simply to right the human balance. The empowering effect on society cannot be overstated. In a world trembling on the brink of nuclear disaster, surely we need to turn away from militaristic imagery and toward the female, nonviolent image of God.[83]

People with a strong sense of human justice think it is natural to honor God as both male and female. Natural images of God as a male/female parent may help us get back in harmony with the world we inhabit. If God can be compared to a woman as well as a man, then no real flesh human being should be categorically subordinated to another on the basis of sex.[84] God the Father is also God the Mother, rising above any disunity. Indeed, all people and all things are reflections of that one all-inclusive divinity. When we speak of God transcending both male and female, the battle of the sexes can end and a new heaven and a new earth can begin.

This loss of the Divine Feminine has endangered civilization and is clearly reflected in the emphasis on conquest and drive for power in modern culture. For the last three thousand years, patriarchal religions have had no image of union and relationship between Goddess and God, no feminine dimension to the Godhead to lend balance and wholeness to our concept of it. The

Divine Feminine is needed to restore wholeness and balance to our image of God and so to ourselves. It is an awakening to a higher level of love, focused beyond individual, family, tribal, or even national concerns. In order to discover this new vision we need to relinquish deeply held scientific and religious beliefs.[85]

The Divine Feminine is initiating a crucial phase in our evolution: urging us to discover a new ethic of responsibility toward the planet, bringing us a new vision of the sacredness and unity of life. Wisdom, justice, beauty, harmony, and compassion are the qualities that have been traditionally identified with the Divine Feminine, yet it is also the irresistible power that destroys the old forms and brings new ones into being, the inspiration of the love-in-action that is so needed to transform a culture radically out of touch with the soul. The Divine Feminine is this unseen dimension of soul to which we are connected through our instincts, our feelings, and the longing imagination of our heart.[86]

11

Thealogy

Thealogy, the study of the divine as Goddess rather than God, has developed into a powerful philosophy that finds expression in many scholarly disciplines, creative arts, and woman-centered activities. Profound questioning about the origin of the species has challenged many traditional assumptions about social roles, including the relationship between men and women, women and religion, and religion and society. Today, everywhere one can see religions, governments and societies led by men. Yet when women looked at prehistoric and ancient cultures, the image of the Great Goddess was everywhere.

The Goddess, as Mother Earth, has been considered supreme in many ancient traditions. Feminist spirituality is a religious system that insists upon the power, value, dignity, and sometimes superiority of women. For the first time, a matriarchal era appears to be based on historical fact, not just political theory. The female Deity is spoken of as the Great Mother, the Great Goddess, Mother God, a symbolic Great Presence, Prime Mover of the Universe, and/or Spark of Creation. Among North American and European women, the veneration of the ancient goddesses of Europe and the Near East has been revived. The varied aspects of the Goddess can shape and influence any culture because it is polytheistic, inclusive, and holistic.[87]

Many thealogists believe that there was a Golden Age that lasted until the Middle Bronze Age, about five thousand years ago, in which women ruled or at least held great social and religious power. Men and women were both free, had control over their bodies and their lives, and lived in harmony with the cosmos. This Golden Age, it is said, was overthrown in Europe and the Mediterranean area by patriarchal Indo-European nomads who killed the priestesses, destroyed the temples of the goddesses, enslaved women, and set up the rule of their father-sky god, the emblem of male domination over women and nature.

Indeed, the idea of the universe as an all-giving Mother has survived into our time. In China, the female deities Ma Tsu and Kuan Yin are still widely worshiped as beneficent and compassionate goddesses. Similarly, the worship of Mary, the Mother of God, is widespread. There are many comforting messages and sightings

coming from Mary all around the world. Mary, representing the Divine Mother, is one of the most revered
figures in the West. Although in Catholic theology she
is demoted to non-divine status, her divinity is implic-
itly recognized by her appellation, Mother of God, as
well as by the prayers of millions who daily seek her
compassionate protection and solace.[88] Millions of
Catholics consider her their spiritual mother.

It must be remembered that not everyone who cel-
ebrates the Goddess has left their church or syna-
gogue and, therefore, invocation of the Goddess did
not always indicate the presence of a new and separate religion. Some of the more radical Christian and
Jewish theology may blend at the edges with thealogy.
Thealogy is a feminist discourse predominantly emergent from a distinct Goddess movement, which has its
own journals and organizes its own events for the celebration of the Goddess and the sharing of insight and
experience. Here the recovery of the Goddess signals
the rebirth of a pre-biblical religion or spirituality perceived by Goddess women to be archaic and native to
all parts of the world. And here, the Goddess is at the
center of the religion, not merely an aspect of a religion
or an attribute of divinity subordinate to higher male
attributes.[89]

Goddess religion and spirituality would not want to be
positioned in such a way as to break its connections to
other traditions. So although Goddess feminism has a

distinctive spiritual/political stamp, it can also be understood as parts of other religions that are considered empowering to women or that already honor female divinities. Goddess feminism is an eclectic, politically driven complex of traditions that adopts and adapts indigenous pagan practices and makes them its own. Sadly, Goddess worship went underground because of the persecution and murder of women who honored her by the Catholic and Protestant churches.[90]

The origin of Goddess feminism can be traced through a history of modern, emancipatory ideas and movements. From the late seventeenth century through the early nineteenth century, Enlightenment and Romantic criticism of government institutions like the Church and the monarchy was to convey egalitarian, anti-authoritarian arguments for the essential dignity of persons regardless of race, gender, property, or class. In the nineteenth century Christian feminism challenged the prevailing ideology that kept women out of the public religious sphere. In the 1960s and 70s, the Women's Liberation movement were empowered to believe it could overturn existing patriarchal institutions. From that time onward, Goddess feminism was born as both a new political stratagem and a new spirituality.[91]

Although most thealogians refer to the Goddess, some see her as a symbol or idea while others see her as a divinity in her own right. Whether she is abstract or functional, she is the symbol and hope of better things to come. All Goddess feminists agree that the Goddess is nature, though she is more than the sum of nature's parts. The Goddess is at least a symbol of collective and individual womanpower, which is itself part of the generative power of nature. She is existence and is therefore available to immediate, self-authenticating, present experience. The reality of the Goddess is inseparable from the reality of the self; she is the process and the fulfillment of the natural self reborn through feminist consciousness.[92]

The Goddess religion is both a very old and a very new phenomenon, as the urge to reinvigorate the sense of God as woman has found its way into mainstream religions. Compared with most other contemporary religions, Goddess feminism is almost newborn. Yet, for Goddess feminists, their religion also has the longest history of all the world's religions. For throughout the world, the worship and symbolism of female divinity seems to have preceded the worship and symbolism of male divinity. Like all religions, however, contemporary Goddess religion must remember its past in order to find and celebrate its present.[93] In establishing a historical continuity between the contemporary revival of the Goddess and the Great Goddess/Mother of the deep past, thealogy offers a potentially global meaning and purpose upon its revival.

12

The Principle of Creation

In the Principle of Creation of Sun Myung Moon's Divine Principle teachings, God embodies both traits of masculinity and femininity, fully harmonized in one creator. God is a being who is the harmonious union of dual characteristics of masculinity and femininity centered on love.[94] It is natural that both femininity and masculinity should reflect the image of God. In general, the masculine language in the Bible has been used to describe the nature of God. In biblical times it was a deeply embedded practice to make women in religion invisible, except as mothers of the sons that carried on the precious lineage. It was miraculous that the Book of Ruth and the Book of Esther even made it into the canonized version of the Old Testament.

The Principle of Creation recognizes that God, as the Parent, Origin, and Creator of everything, reflects the same structure, attributes, and dynamics in the creation. Thus, God should properly be understood as the perfect union of male and female (Heavenly Father and Heavenly Mother), that is, the wellspring of perfect love, namely parental love for all persons and for everything.[95] God is both masculine and feminine, perfectly harmonized in one eternal Being, that is, God is the harmonious union of masculinity and femininity.[96]

As our invisible, internal Parent, God created human beings as His/Her substantial children. Adam and Eve were created in the image of God, as the substantial object partners to God in the pattern of His/Her dual characteristics. As God's first substantial partners, they were meant to be the Parents of humankind. They were meant to become husband and wife, bear and raise children, and from a family manifest the true love of parents, the true love of husband and wife, and the true love of children.[97]

Everything in creation exists because of a reciprocal relationship between the dual characteristics of positivity and negativity. The fact that everything exists in positive and negative pairs clarifies that God exists with dual characteristics of positivity and negativity or masculinity and femininity. These pairs are polar opposites that complement each other and at the same time attract each other. Opposite characteristics of man/woman, male/female, and plus/minus attract each other, forming a bond and generating energy that produces new life.

Establishing masculinity and femininity in the heart of God and hence promoting the view that the masculine heart of men and the feminine heart of women are distinct yet absolute in value would offer new foundations for pursuing equality between men and women. Establishing the feminine heart of God as corresponding with the masculine heart of God could help to increase the recognition of Mother God, where God's Masculinity and Femininity are equally appreciated by God, humanity, and the creation. Acknowledgment of the heart of Mother God, similar to the heart of Father God, although distinct, is vital. Understanding this will enhance the self-image of women and men, empowering both as they may be able better to visualize and appreciate the powerful and loving Mother God, who supports them in pursuing enhanced roles in the pursuit of peace.[98] It has been said, by more than one medium, that when we die and go to the spirit world, we will experience a Heavenly Father and a Heavenly Mother.

Matriarchy and patriarchy are two fundamental and opposing ways of life in this world and understanding reality. They are all-pervasive and deeply affect our perception of reality.[99] In understanding the nature of God, perhaps a constructive synthesis would combine the experiences of matriarchy and patriarchy and see God as both male and female. Similarly, the concept of an androgynous God has been advanced in mystical writings and appeared in ancient Greece as well.

Androgyny restores women to a major position in the Godhead without alienating men. The dual characteristics of God are a divine Father and Mother, who were to be united as one in Adam and Eve.[100]

The fact that God possesses both masculinity and femininity makes Him/Her a being of dual characteristics. Each person is God's substantial object partner who manifests a distinctive aspect of God's dual characteristics.[101] Therefore, the nature of God embodies the traits of masculinity/femininity that are fully harmonized in one Creator. The creation of man and woman in the image of God carries the implication that God, as the source and model for both man and woman, should contain within His/Her being feminine qualities such as nurturing, responsiveness, and mercy as well as masculine qualities such as strength, purposefulness and judgment. God blended all the male attributes within Himself to create man, and all the female attributes within Herself to create woman.[102]

13

Insights on Mother God's Nature

Our world is not overflowing with information about the love of God in the feminine. Just how often in history is the femininity of God expressed? How often in Scriptures or holy texts are there instances of God speaking to women? Understanding and recognizing the female aspects of God is something new for most people. Nonetheless, how normal is a gender-balanced divine Father and Mother God. Can a new life be born without both a father and a mother? Mother God wants to parent her children because She is capable of what no human can do. She is asking everyone to have faith and trust in Her, in the femininity of God. Most people still don't know that the divided masculine and feminine responsibilities of God are in full force to love humanity.

Human beings have to break past habits and come to terms with the true identity of God. They have to learn a new tradition of trusting, even unconditionally, a Divine Mother. Still, most people do not understand that God might refer to Herself as She. How and when will humanity be able to make jump to celebrate both God's femininity and God's masculinity? God's real problem has been the heartache of separation and the terrible loss and pain in lives of her children spent in unhappiness, without resolution. She is asking everyone to have faith in her true identity. With only a handful of people informed enough to care for others, Mother God has been reduced to working in extremely limited ways. In fact, contrary to what most people think, She is actually under-resourced.

In time, many people will be asking, "Mother God, where have you been?" We are present at a time when the world is dying and waiting to be reborn, and all the words in our libraries and on the Internet cannot tell us what to do. If we learn to listen we will discover that life, the Great Mother, is speaking to us, telling us what we need to know. The sacred feminine can share with us her secrets, tell us how to be, how to midwife Her rebirth. The Divine Feminine is asking us to be present in life in all of its wholeness, without judgment or plans. And because we are her children she can speak to each one of us, if we have the humility to listen.[103]

Today as people seek for a more fulfilling relationship with God, they are drawn to God's feminine nature. The Divine Feminine can be appealed to for help,

guidance, and inspiration at any time. It is even becoming more common to pray to God as Heavenly
Mother. This religious revolution is so subtle yet so
widespread that her arrival is sure to change the way
the world looks at God and one another. There have
been many insights from all parts of the world as to the
feminine or motherly aspect of God. Here are some
notable quotations about her appearance and coming:

> The Age of Aquarius has been defined as an astro-
> logical era, or a great cosmic cycle in the spiritual
> evolution of our consciousness. This age is intended
> to bring about a spiritual transformation and heal-
> ing unlike any other. It is the age when our aware-
> ness of God as Mother and Holy Spirit comes to
> the forefront. This is the age of the Divine Mother
> and the Holy Spirit. The Divine Mother, called the
> Universal Mother or Cosmic Virgin, is the feminine
> polarity of the Godhead. She is the "other side" of
> Father. In the East she is known as Kuan Yin, the
> Chinese Goddess of Mercy and Compassion and
> in the West as Mary, Mother of Jesus. These are
> only two of her manifestations. Being multi-faced,
> the Divine Mother has a thousand and one faces
> and reflection is constantly changing. The concept
> of the Divine Mother embraces yet transcends all
> religions.[104]

> The Goddess is Mother Earth, who sustains all
> growing things, who is the body, our bones and

cells. She is air – the winds that move in the trees and over the waves, breath. She is the fires of the hearth, the blazing bonfire and the fuming volcano, the power of transformation and change. And she is water – the sea, original source of life, the rivers streams, lakes and wells; the blood that flows in the rivers of our veins. She is mare, cow, owl, crane, flower, tree, apple, seed, lion, sow, stone, woman. She is found in the world around us, in the cycles and seasons of nature, in mind, body, spirit, and emotions within each of us. [105]

Divine feminine energy is comprised of the following divine, angelic qualities - unconditional love, understanding, compassion, nurturing, and helpfulness to others. It includes tenderness, gentleness, kindness and all the other divine feelings you might relate to unconditional love - the greatest of all God's divine cosmic powers. The unconditional love within divine feminine energy has a powerful magnetic quality. At its highest levels of 5th and 6th dimensional conscious Oneness with God, unconditional love has the power to heal, to harmonize, and to create miracles just as Jesus did so long ago.[106]

She is the mighty and wise One who opens us to the supramental infinities and the cosmic vastness, to the grandeur of the supreme Light, to a treasurehouse of miraculous knowledge, to the measureless movement of the Mother's eternal forces. Tranquil is she and wonderful, great and calm forever, Nothing can move her because all wisdom is in her; nothing is hidden from her that she chooses to know; she comprehends all things and all beings and their nature and what moves them and the law of the world and it times and how all was and is and must be. A strength is in her that masters everything and none can prevail against her vast intangible wisdom and high tranquil power.[107]

There are four great aspects of the Mother. One is her personality of calm wideness, comprehending wisdom, inexhaustible compassion and all-ruling majesty. The second embodies her power of splendid strength, irresistible passion, warrior mood, her overwhelming will, her impetuous swiftness and world-shaking force. A third is vivid, sweet, beautiful, harmonious rhythm, her intricate subtle opulence, her compelling attraction and her captivating grace. The fourth is her profound capacity of intimate knowledge, her quiet flawless work and her exact perfection of all things.[108]

The Goddess can only be perceived as manifested. She is thus, in herself, the divine or cosmic power, the first and absolute cause of all existence. She is endlessly creating new forms, undulations, vibrations, that emanate from a central point in a limitless universe.[109] One fact remains certain: the permanence, throughout the millennia, of a mysterious goddess, whose concrete representations vary according to the period, but who is always ambivalent, generator of life and death, and also a transforming power, since she presides over the passage from the visible world to the invisible world.[110]

The divine feminine is the revelation of the hidden God. She is divinity proposing, revealing, creating, assisting, and alluring: she is also the inner dynamism of the world obeying, receiving, responding, and cooperating. Through her the heavens declare the glory of God, the prophets are overshadowed by the living Light, and the faithful participate in the Virtues. Her bearing is regal toward the cosmos, erotic toward God, maternal toward men and women, her epiphanies aim to inspire the love of wisdom through the beauty of holiness. She is the faithful mirror of divine intentions but also of human actions; it is her vesture that men and women adorn through good works or disfigure through sin.[111]

Since Mother God is the overall earth ruler, She can dart in and out and be wherever She needs to be.[112] Let's say you are having financial problems or a lawsuit. Mother God will interfere with you and help you with this, if you petition her. You may say, "Why would I petition Mother God for money matters? Because she can interfere, that's why! She is the crusader against negative energy. Visualize her standing in front of you with Her beautiful golden sword, who can literally take the brunt of any negative energy. She can handle anything.[113]

At the end of his life, Aurobindo is said to have remarked, "If there is to be a future, it will wear the crown of feminine design." The Mother is the all-willing, all-loving, all powerful, at once the ground, energy and goal of evolution. There is no end or limit imaginable to her love or its transforming powers. In her and in them, and in our working consciously, directly, and humbly with her and them, is our great human hope.[114] What he saw and knew from his own experience was that if we could align ourselves totally and passionately in love and dedication to the Divine Mother, it could transform all aspects of human life. It could transform not only our minds, illuminated by the ecstasy of the divine gnosis of the Mother; not only our hearts, opened to the unconditional love of the Mother; it would open our vision to the light coursing through all the various chakras and blazing above our heads.[115]

14

When God Was a Woman

In prehistoric and early historic periods of human development, religions existed in which people revered their supreme creator as female. This Great Goddess had been worshiped from the beginning of the Neolithic period. Some authorities would extend Goddess worship as far into the past as the Upper Paleolithic Age of about 25,000 BC. For thousands of years both matriarchal and patriarchal religions existed simultaneously – among closely neighboring peoples. Archaeological, mythological, and historical evidence all reveal that the female religion, far from naturally fading away, was the victim of centuries of continual persecution and suppression by the advocates of the newer religions that held male deities as supreme. Most of the artifacts concerning the vast female religion, which flourished for thousands of years before the advent of Judaism, Christianity, and the Classical

Age of Greece, have been dug out of the ground only to be reburied in obscure archaeological texts, carefully shelved away in the exclusively protected stacks of university and museum libraries. In nearly every Neolithic and historic excavation there are discoveries of temples of the Goddess. Most of the art during prehistoric times made its appearance in the form of animal carvings and statuettes of the supreme deity, the Mother Goddess.[116] Antagonistic attitudes of the Abrahamic religions may have caused much of this ancient material to be intentionally destroyed.[117]

A consciousness of the relationship of the veneration of the Goddess to the matrilineal descent of name, property, and the rights to the throne is vital in understanding the suppression of the Goddess religion.[118] There is little doubt that female kinship customs and the reverence of the female deity was the underlying reason for the resentment of the worship of the Goddess by patriarchal invaders. The people who believed in male deities held a superior attitude over female deities, which often led to the suppression of Goddess worship. The female religions, especially after the earlier invasions, appear to have assimilated the male deities into the older worship, and the Goddess survived as the popular religion of the people for thousands of years after the initial invasions.[119] If the majority of the population once held the Goddess as sacred, it does not seem too surprising to find that these beliefs were revived at times when it was safe to do so openly.

Myths, statutes, and documentary evidence reveal the continual presence of the Goddess and the survival of the customs and rituals connected to its religion, despite the efforts of conquerors to destroy or belittle the ancient worship.[120] The status and origins of the Great Goddess have been the subject of a number of studies of ancient worship. The archaeological artifacts suggest that in all the Neolithic and early Chalcolithic societies, the Divine Ancestress, generally referred to by most writers as the Mother Goddess, was revered as the supreme deity.[121] Throughout the Near and Middle East, the Goddess was celebrated in primeval times. From 3,000 BC onward, priestesses had been portrayed in sculptures and appeared in murals and other artifacts of Crete, for example, strongly suggesting that it was women who controlled the worship.[122]

For thousands of years the sexual customs of the Goddess religion and the sexual autonomy of women generally had helped women to retain their independence economically, socially, and legally. It seems to have been the very nature of the sexual customs, so inherent and integral a part of the female religion, allowing for and possibly encouraging matrilineal descent patterns to continue, that aroused the most violent reactions among the Levite patrilinealists.[123] The sexual autonomy of women in the religion of the Goddess posed a continual threat to the far-reaching goals of men. The influence of these ancient religions was a constant problem, as described in the Old Testament.

The Levite writers labeled any sexually autonomous women as whores and harlots and demanded the enforcement of their own patriarchal attitudes concerning the sexual ownership of women.[124]

Examining the documentary evidence proves undeniably the chronology of supremacy of the female deity to its eventual suppression. Invading Hebrews gaining control of land and governments eventually destroyed more than a few matrilineal systems. Though buried deep beneath the sands of what was once Canaan, statues of the female deity have been unearthed in archaeological excavations. These images of the Goddess, some dating back as far as 7,000 BC, offer silent testimony to the most ancient worship of the Queen of Heaven in the land that is today most often remembered as the birthplace of both Judaism and Christianity.[125] The religion of the Goddess was a great temptation for the Hebrews who had invaded Canaan since, for many of them, it may have been the religion of their ancestors.

Despite the various methods used to confuse the identity and gender of the Goddess as Ashtoreth or Asherah, even in the Bible as we know it today, passages and symbolism betray the influential and prevailing presence of the ancient worship of the female deity, while other Canaanite and Near Eastern artifacts confirm it.[126] Many Bible passages report that idols of the female deity, referred to as Asherah, were to be found on every hill, under every green tree, and alongside altars in the temples. The worship of the Goddess as Ashtoreth was widespread through the Mediterranean area.[127] Religions of the Goddess and a female kinship system were closely intertwined in many parts of the Near East. There is no doubt that in biblical periods of Canaan, the Levite priests of the Hebrews were in continual contact with the religion of the Goddess. The followers of Yahweh destroyed the shrines of the female deity wherever they could, murdering when they could not convert.[128]

The civilizations that worshiped the Goddess, which had flourished for thousands of years, bringing with them in earliest time inventions in methods of agriculture, medicine, architecture, metallurgy, wheeled vehicles, ceramics, textiles and written languages were gradually stamped out.[129] Commands for the destruction of the religion of the Goddess were built into the very canons and laws of the male religions that replaced it. With the gradual acceptance of the male religions, premarital virginity and marital fidelity for women were incorporated into the attitudes and laws of the societies which embraced them. The new male deity was designed, constructed and propagated to "keep women in their place."

Much of the writing of the Old Testament was adopted into the sacred literature of Christianity. The writers and religious leaders who followed Christ assumed the same pose of contempt for the female, continuing to use religion to lock women further into the role of passive and inferior beings, and thus more easily controlled as property of men. As the years went on and the position and status of women continued to lose ground, the Church held fast to its goals of creating and maintaining a male-dominated society.[130] Dogma, statements, and edicts were carefully designed to suppress women's rights. Within the very structure of the contemporary male religions are the laws and attitudes originally designed to annihilate the female religions, female sexual authority, and matrilineal descent.

For hundreds of generations male supremacy has been suggested, declared, proven, explained, announced, affirmed, and reaffirmed by those who believed in the Bible as the sacred word of the Creator. Yet the memory of some elements of the ancient female religion – the Queen of Heaven, the priestesses, the sacred sexual customs – still lingers on in the memory of some of the men who control the Church even today.[131] The facts about the early female religions should be brought to light as they have been hidden away too long. This will help in clearing away centuries of confusion, misunderstanding, and suppression so that ultimately the Divine Feminine can be recognized.

15

The Goddess Re-Awakening

The Goddess has slept in the unconscious for thousands of years. She has periodically awakened, and images of her have emerged – wonderful images of great power and beauty, and also of great power and destructiveness. The rediscovery of the Goddess not only involves the development of new ideas, new symbols, new rituals, maybe new religions, but a reappraisal of the past. Thus, throughout the history of the Christian Church there have been rich veins of feminine spirituality and mysticism, often ignored or demeaned, that we are able to reevaluate today as manifestations of the slumbering Goddess.[132]

The ancient images of the Goddess have allowed us to reconstruct core concepts of the feminine principle. Over the last two decades more and more women have been discovering the Goddess as she had been known and worshiped in many cultures around the world. Women have been questioning what has kept them from being who they really wanted to be and doing what they really wanted to do. Women are now reconsidering and challenging the role that mainstream religions have played in keeping them in subordinate roles. It reminds us of ancient traditions developed in societies where women were not dominated by men but were central to the social and spiritual values that honored life.[133]

Throughout the long journey of life on earth, there has never been a time or place that did not include the female aspect of God. To heal and revive our world and all the people in it, we need to look again at the older religious traditions that sought and followed a concept of a female God. The Divine She, the Mother Earth and Queen of Heaven, the She of the underworld, all express a concept that has been swept from patriarchal thought and tradition. Only in this way can women's "thirteenth hour" help humanity survive the crisis that male imbalance has brought upon the created world.[134]

The Buddhist, Hindu, Egyptian, Greek and Roman female deities have greatly guided cultures for a long time. From hunting to healing to dreaming, the presence of the Goddesses influenced ancient life from birth to death. However, they were ruthlessly suppressed by early Christian patriarchs. As a result, Christian women have lacked a positive image of their own innate divinity and healing power.[135] Under patriarchy, women healers have been denigrated and even burned at the stake as agents of the devil instead of being revered as embodiments of the Goddess and channels of her healing power.

Is it just coincidental that, in our time, we are also regaining our ecological consciousness, that there are modern movements for social and economic justice, that equality, development, and peace are three interrelated goals of the first United Nations Decade for Women, and that there is a re-awakening of the awareness that nature and spirituality are inextricably intertwined? Although new age Goddess spirituality is viewed with caution, feminist spirituality continues to flourish in art, drama, poetry, psychology and fiction writing.

There is incompleteness in ourselves and in our history. We sense the absence of the suppressed feminine half. We need the Goddess now because she illuminates aspects of divinity that are left out of patriarchal religions. But the incompleteness we seek to rectify as we reinstate the Goddess is in our culture and our language, not in the Divine. The female half is not missing from God; it is missing from our picture of God.[136]

To be of ultimate service to the planet, we must reconnect to that innate feminine knowing that teaches us of the power of change that comes from being rather than knowing. Feminine qualities belong to both men and women, and they draw us into the depths within us. They also connect us with the primal pain of the feminine that has been abused by our masculine culture. We come to experience her tears and wounds, her pain that is also the pain of our own soul. The feminine consciousness within all of life needs our attention in order to redeem civilization and our world. Her cry needs to be heard, her knowing brought into our consciousness. Our masculine culture has focused on the external, but the feminine knows a different dimension – that which is hidden within.

Male strength was at a premium in the industrial society that has long passed its peak and is on the way out in the West. Those hierarchies of dominion are universally breaking down. People refuse to be ruled in an autocratic way. We are in a changeover period of seeming chaos because the new post-industrial society has not settled down yet from the ferment. Female ways of doing things are coming into their own – nurturing, relating, and interconnecting in networks – not possessed by females alone but by women and men in partnership.[137]

The feminine holds the mystery of the creation. This simple and primordial truth is often overlooked, but at this time of global crisis, which also carries the seeds of global transformation, we need to reawaken to the spiritual power and potential of the feminine. Without the feminine, nothing new can come into existence – we will remain caught in the materialistic images of life that are polluting our planet and desecrating our souls. We need to return to the core of our being, to where the sacred comes into existence. And the mystical feminine holds the key to this work of redemption and transformation.[138]

16

Is It OK to Call God, "Mother"?

When looking at history, scripture or linguistics, different systems of interpretation can produce extremely different results. Many generations did not see sexism in scripture because their experience was so clouded by patriarchal cultural attitudes. The incomplete concept of the God that was once exclusively male is presently becoming one that encompasses and transcends masculinity and femininity. Many of the saints down through the ages have recognized the motherhood of God, and they are joined by an increasing number of those today who sing the praises of the God who is both Mother and Father.[139] The qualities of both a mother and father coexist in perfect balance and harmony in God. Until we grasp this, the same balance and harmony will continue to elude us in humankind because sexism destroys the visibility of both the divine and the human feminine.[140]

Some of the earliest orthodox Christian references to mother-father God occur in the second century writings of Clement of Alexandria. In *Christ the Educator*, Clement understands Mother as the aspect of God's nature that has empathy with humankind. In the early fifth century the Bishop of Ptolemais in Lyby, Synesius, said of God, "You are Father, You are Mother, You are Male, and You are Female." Mechtild of Magdeburg (1210-1280), a nun and teacher of the church, said, "God is not only fatherly. God is also a mother who lifts her loved child from the ground to her knee." Julian of Norwich (1342-1423), a saintly and influential Christian writer wrote often of God as both Father and Mother using such phrases as: "As truly as God is our Father, so is truly God our Mother" and "God almighty is our loving Father, and God all wisdom is our loving Mother."[141] The power of a gender-balanced metaphor is seen in a beautiful passage from Psalms (Ps.123:2) that depicts us as God's servants and God as a man or a woman in charge of our lives and upon whom we can depend.[142] Naming God in both male and female terms demonstrates the equality of women and men and calls our patriarchal society into question as nothing else can.

The brokenness resulting from the masculine and feminine divide in our world today directly affects many areas of life, ranging from the "glass ceiling" in the workplace to the stained glass ceiling in our churches. It includes absent and confused fathers and harassed single mothers. One out of every six people in the United States is living in poverty, and most of them are women and children. Most people do not understand how theology is inescapably intertwined with social and political actions.[143] Sexism, like racism, is evil, inhuman, and anti-Christian. Limiting ourselves to male leadership and predominantly masculine images of God is a disservice to men as well as women. It denies a part of ourselves, regardless of the way in which a culture defines masculinity or femininity. The Christian community is deformed to the extent it practices the injustice of sexism.[144]

Underlying the challenge of how men and women are to relate is the image of God.[145] The sheer magnitude of the repetition of masculine words prevents any other image from getting a foothold. On top of that, gender distortions about God may produce feelings of fear, sexual abuse, abandonment, and a pervasive sense that God can't be trusted. To become both fully human and fully divine, we all need an emotional dimension of a parental relationship with God, which is like getting the best from a super-healthy father and a super-healthy mother. Since the purpose and rules appear to have changed, some new guidelines about how men and women should interact would be appropriate.

There is usually a period of culture shock that people go through when they are introduced to the feminine language about God. Becoming comfortable with the feminine language of God seems unreal at first. Becoming comfortable with the feminine language of God seems unreal at first. This new "face" of God is different from the culturally conditioned emotions and habit patterns we are used to. Eventually calling God Father and Mother will seem less heretical and more orthodox than those who would limit God to only Father.[146] In order to expand our image of God, one has to remove the maleness of God dominating the femaleness of God. This false image is a dangerous one because it provides the underlying rationale for male supremacy and violence against women. As long as women are seen as inferior, evil, and sexually seductive, it will be impossible to see the feminine of God.[147]

The war on women is not a war of men against women. We naively assume that this war has been declared by and caused by men. It is being fought against both sexes, against all of us. In this war, women have lost the feeling of power, and men have lost the power of feeling. Women have lost their confidence in the public sphere and men have lost it in the private family sphere. Men have won the illusion of control. Women have won the illusion of security. If we assign stereotypical qualities to each gender, then both men and women have each lost half of their humanity.[148]

An attitude of patriarchy is fundamentally at the root of a culture that allows women to be beaten and abused. Violence against women, including assault, mutilation, murder, infanticide, rape, and neglect, is one of the most pervasive, yet unrecognized evils in the world. The pervasive evil of patriarchy is given legitimacy by the idea of a primarily male or masculine God. Where male is valued over female, women suffer not only psychological damage but physical abuse and death as male violence toward women continues in crisis proportions all over the world today.[149]

We must face the facts: there is a war on women. The collateral physical and mental damage to humanity and the planet is incalculable. This undeclared war on women is the longest running, most destructive, and most pervasive war on earth. While the war on women has been waged for centuries all over the planet, only recently has the existence of this war been seriously acknowledged, named, and openly challenged.[150] Most people are still oblivious to it and don't even see how they participate in it. Christians have especially sanctified this battle by claiming it was God's idea from the beginning of creation.[151] Centuries of assault on the nurturing, maternal, and compassionate images of God have resulted in the virtual abortion of the feminine in much of the church today. This dismemberment and discarding of the feminine in leadership and language is the most pressing theological and social agenda within the church today. The abortion of the feminine from our language about God is the foundation of the war against women within the church, which is why calling God Mother is an important first step toward a solution.[152]

A fundamental part of our disease is the alienation of masculine and feminine not only in humankind and in the image of God, but within each of us individually. Deeply buried traumatic incidents from the past, repeated abusive treatment, and unmet needs from our childhood, if unhealed, cause great emotional pain and reduce our capacity to function. Inner healing deals with the wounding of the inner self from childhood. Good psychology recognizes how crucial it is to receive both maternal and paternal love from our earthly parents. What they don't realize is that we also need paternal and maternal love from our Heavenly Parent.[153]

A growing number of both men and women are beginning to perceive the reality of our sexist theological, political, and social structures. Thinking people realize that oppression of any group is actually the oppression of us all. Contemporary people are more interested in a true, egalitarian spirituality and not one that is stuck in the culturally defined patriarchal patterns of the past. Every aspect of our lives - romance, social relationships, marriage, business, church, and family - is being called into question as patriarchy crumbles and women come into their own liberated womanhood. The old models don't work and actually never did.[154]

It is naive to deny the pervasive social, legal, and even religious framework that promotes this violence against women. One part of that framework is the insistence by Christians that God is primarily masculine. One's picture of God validates certain attitudes and confronts others. Men have reported that including God's feminine side has had an interesting effect on their attitudinal violence against women. When men see the feminine in God, they value women more, and it becomes more difficult to treat them in demeaning ways. Changing our language and incorporating the feminine image of God are critical components of changing our attitude and patterns of violence toward women.[155]

The only way to get to true manhood is by first rejecting the false version of male domination. Perhaps one of the most profound changes in this journey comes when we abandon the old patriarchal divine images and come alive to God as Woman – mother, sister, grandmother, friend, and lover. Until we understand the feminine side of God we don't know how to embrace the masculine side without getting entangled again in the old patriarchal images of divinity.[156]

There is a centuries-old wounding that cries out to be touched. Men and women have waited all their lives to have the feminine face of God recognized and affirmed, and when it was, they were healed. Many are not aware how the imagery in the Bible, with its rigid role definitions, is embedded in our psyches. We must allow time for new perspectives to sink in as we come into a deeper consciousness of God's image.[157] The ignorance of the feminine side of God prevents us from looking into the mothering eyes of God. At the deepest level, the image of God is not only an issue of truth but also one of deep inner healing.[158] Advocating God as Mother frees us up to embrace God as Father in even more credible and healthy ways.

17

The Feminine Dimension of the Divine

Today many faithful from all over the world are looking for deeper and more meaningful ways of understanding their spirituality. In fact, there is a growing desire on the part of men and women for access to the Divine Feminine. In the last twenty-five years there has been an outpouring of books and articles generated by the search to understand the feminine nature of God. Through searching the scriptures for hidden meaning, new linguistic translations, anthropological finding and historic studies, inspirational awareness of the Divine Femininity is surfacing. Not only do a multitude of divine images reflect scriptural use, but perhaps these new developments will enable us to see beyond our one-sided tradition to a less pretentious Christianity, one which can bring a more balanced, healing message to our diverse world.[159]

The expression of Sophia as Mother God existed in the Judeo-Christian tradition since the fourth century BC. By the beginning of the Christian era, Sophia was portrayed in history and assuming the roles of judge and savior of the Jewish people. Her stature and importance rivaled the power of Yahweh himself. However, within a hundred years, Sophia's power was broken and she was superseded by a masculine figure who took over her roles. The early Christians replaced her with Jesus and within a few decades of his crucifixation, all her powers and attributes had been ascribed to Christ. As a result of this transference of attributes, overt access to the feminine dimension of the divine in the Judeo-Christian tradition was cut off or repressed. This laid the groundwork for the return of the great feminine archetypes in disguised and hidden forms in the theology of the early Church.[160]

The history of Mother Mary takes us even further into the mystery of the Mother aspect of God. There is little doubt that the archetypal Great Mother has appeared in the image of Mary. Although theologically she is not a deity, existentially, psychologically, symbolically, she is a Goddess, an image of feminine sublimity and transcendence.[161] Through adoring Mary we become one with her, grow something of her Mother-power and Mother-spirit in ourselves, and come through grace to participate in her life of joy and glory. This is not theology; this is experience. Mary can do anything, if we let her, and will, if we open to her as she is always open to us – simply, naturally, tenderly, completely. The great reward of knowing her in this all-healing intimacy is to find out she is closer to us than our jugular vein.[162]

Mary's role as mother was also important to early Church Fathers. She was regarded as the mother of all Christians. By the fifth century Mary was called the Mother of God to reinforce this orthodox position. The purpose of glorifying Mary was to increase glorification of her son, Jesus. However, Mary emerged as a powerful figure in her own right, with many attributes formerly associated with the Hellenistic goddesses. Clearly this is an example of the return of the repressed feminine, which found a weak spot. Yet Mariology has archetypal qualities that are distorted. Mary is always referred to as a creature, and the attributes assigned to her are one-dimensional. Her theology is fraught with conflicting messages and the images that result are confused. She both is and is not a goddess or a representative of the feminine dimension of the divine.[163]

The Great Mother archetype continues to manifest in different ways across different cultures. All goddesses with their associated symbols and attributes are cultural representations of these archetypes. The importance of a mother's presence in history, in both a literal and a figurative sense, cannot be understated. Figures of the Great Goddesses are represented in the myths and artistic creations of mankind. So much so that it appears as an archetype of the collective unconscious.

This archetype then emerges into consciousness, where it finds expression as a Great Goddess. Thus the goddess is an appropriate aspect of the divine for all people, in all places, and at all times, and not merely in pagan or primitive cultures.[164]

18

The Great Cosmic Mother

In the world's oldest creation myths, the female god creates the world out of her own body. The Great Mother was the active and autonomous Creatrix of the world. The ancient Goddess was always there – alive, immanent – within her creation.[165] The first arts and religions, the first crafts and social patterns, were designed in recognition and celebration of her. The religious beliefs, the mysteries and rites developed by ancient women grew organically out of women's supreme roles as cultural producers, mothers, and prime communicators with the spirit world.[166] According to folklore tradition, the ancient Great Mother of all living gave birth parthenogenetically, to herself and the entire cosmos. She was the world egg, containing the two halves of all polarities or dualism - the yin/yang of continuity and change, expansion and contraction of the universe. Ancient as this cosmology is, it remains the most accurate statement of cosmic process yet made. The concept of a female earth as the source of cyclic birth, life, death, and rebirth underlies all mythological and religious symbology. The Goddess of the Neolithic became the teacher of planting, harvesting, and storage methods, as well as healer and dispenser of curative herbs, roots, and plants.[167] The first God, Mother Earth, a human response to an experienced fact as the original and sustaining force of the universe, was always considered female. Modern physicists have only been able to confirm these ancient conceptions of how the universe creates and recreates itself.[168]

The earliest human ancestors' anthropological and archaeological evidence substantiates what many people may not know: the first "God" was female. Evidence shows that some of the most advanced societies of the ancient world – technologically as well as culturally advanced – were matrifocal, i.e., woman oriented, led by women and worshipers of a Goddess. The mysteries of female biology dominated human religious and artistic thought, as well as social organization, for at least the first 200,000 years of human life on earth.[169] An essential trait of matriarchal societies was that they were peaceful and affirmed life. Prehistoric (Neolithic) societies were relatively egalitarian, without hierarchy, exploitation, or marked aggression. The Great Goddess kept her supremacy throughout the Mediterranean, the Aegean, Turkey and the Near East, Northwest Africa and Europe through Neolithic times, until the very end - the Bronze Age - though in changing forms.[170]

Somehow, God as Father is not of the same all-containing, all-infusing, and nourishing nature as Mother God, and so the relation between humans and Father God became abstract, alienated, distant, and moralistic. The Father's way in all the patriarchal world religions is separate from the world and from us. It was absolute, good, and right but static. Patriarchal law, often called "the Will of God," is in fact wholly secular, cynical, and legally designed purposely to maintain male power through institutional control of female energy. With patriarchal legal, religious, and economic-social systems, all men benefited from their organized domination of the community of women.[171] Essentially, order everywhere meant the suppression and negation of the Great Mother religion.

The settled people of the Old Testament, like everyone else in the Near East, practiced Goddess worship. The Old Testament is the record of the conquest and massacre of Neolithic people by the nomadic Hebrews, who then set up their biblical God in place of the ancient Goddess.[172] The Levite priesthood was intent on instituting patrilineal property and inheritance rights based on women's total submission and spiritual disinheritance. Any autonomy by women was seen as a threat to their new command. Women's rights were reversed and they had to undergo a God-willed social, physical and spiritual oppression that continues to this day. The current patriarchal systems have not done the human soul justice. From its beginning in mass bloodshed, repression, and plunder, it has for four millennia robbed and exploited the energies of the earth and her creatures.[173] As a result of the Semitic people invading the world of the Mother Goddess, the male-oriented theologies became dominant, causing the end of the Mother Goddess systems that had maintained thousands of years of culture unbroken by war.

The corruption of the original yin/yang oracular-mystical system into a dualistic system of hierarchy, dominance, and oppression occurred, in the East as in the West, in the shift of human culture from land-tribal to court-hierarchic, i.e., in the shift from matrifocal-rural to patrifocal-urban social structures.[174] Male deities rose to power over the Great Goddess gradually but sometimes quickly. The sun cult, the worship of the Sun God and an all-male priesthood, was typically established, as in Babylon and Egypt, by the edict of a military dictatorship.[175] To accommodate the new beliefs, all the religious and cultural values were transferred from female control to male. Many epics, myths, and folktales describe the breaking up of old established matriarchal world orders with ferocious conquests and formidable iron weaponry. Patriarchal religion was then used as an internal mechanism of oppression. The pattern was repeated everywhere. History was literally being re-written from her-story to his-story.

Tragically, God the Father was perceived to be the enemy of the Mother God. Yet there appeared many messianic individuals and movements that were like children of the Great Mother, struggling to balance society with a dual outlook, only to be persecuted through organized religion, i.e., the Inquisition. It was the male priesthoods of Father God religions who first wrote and enforced the new laws and new customs that stripped Neolithic women of all their ancient sexual autonomy and made their sexual and reproductive functions the property of a dominating male elite – for God and for profit.[176] The Neolithic Goddess religions that had supported female sexual autonomy – female control over both sexual pleasure and reproduction – were religiously demonized and politically destroyed.[177] In fact, all present political, economic, social, and religious systems on earth are built solidly on the fact of female weakness.[178] Consequently, the past four thousand years have resulted in almost total physical and ideological suppression of the female.

19

The Myth of the Evil Feminine

The five hundred years of the European Inquisition were a systematic and intensive punishment of the female soul. The church thought women were by nature agents and tools of the devil. Witchcraft was why the church allowed Joan of Arc to be burned. Condemnation, torture, and killings occurred in public and were sanctified by the Church. Of the one million to nine million people burned as witches, 80 percent of those accused and burnt were women. Town records from Germany and France reveal that whole villages were emptied of their female populations during the peak of the fire-frenzy – including very young girls and very elderly women.[179]

The myth of a malignant image of the male-female relationship and of the nature of women is still deeply imbedded in the modern psyche. The myth has affected doctrines and laws that concern women's status in society, and it has contributed to biased male-centered ethical theories. The myth also undergirds destructive patterns in the fabric of our culture. It influences literature, the mass media, social customs, and social laws. Most ironically, the discrimination women have experienced is a corruption and denial of the Christian gospel.

Society supported these religious beliefs and practices, even when it might have meant disobeying the message of its respective founders. Women have been marginalized, denied important roles, and made subordinate to men in all things. But if women can come to know the sacred dimension of their own and the earth's suffering, if they can see that it is part of the mysterious destiny of the soul of our world, if they can look beyond their own personal pain and anger to accept their larger destiny, then the forces of life can flow in a new way.

There has been a "great silence" about not only women's accomplishments under patriarchy but about women's historical existence and influence before the dawn of patriarchy. Despite archaeological discoveries and a variety of research writings proving a former feminine preeminence, history books were written with little or no mention of a matriarchal period. In addition, science has done little to educate the general population that, although men and women have different abilities, in order to fulfill their differing roles, one is not inferior or superior to the other. Equality between the sexes should be incorporated in educational protocol, political representation, business activity, public life, and most important – family life.

The damage from the myth of the evil feminine is untold and unimaginable. For a long time in the past, and even today, genital mutilation, female infanticide, and the mistreatment of girls has been common. Childless women were denigrated and often divorced. Widows were denied remarriage and had to live a miserable existence. Meanwhile, men could indulge their sexual needs extramaritally if not permitted to marry more than one wife. Men had the right to divorce and were favored in inheritance and property rights. Women's legal rights, including marriage rights, the right to vote, child custody, and employment opportunities, often lagged far behind men's. The major tool used to suppress the progress of females has been the denial of education.[180] Political, business, and personal freedoms were stifled and limited by male-dominated authorities who dictated the policies and practices of society. The myth of male superiority has had a major effect on human behavior that continues to this day.

It is hard not to wonder what course history and women's lives would have taken if they had been accepted as equals. Of late, women have made rapid progress within a short period of time toward equality in education and employment, especially in Europe and North America. Female education became generally available in the Western world in the last two hundred years, following many millennia of denial. Standards of living and all the advances we have witnessed in the last century in science and industry might well have been realized much earlier. National prosperities would have been more advanced, birth-rates lower, and local and national conflicts less frequent. Countries that still deny women equality in this day and age should understand it is unlikely they can compete and make progress while over half their citizens are unproductive.[181]

The universal and irrational belief that there is a repugnant element in femaleness reflects man's underlying fear and dread of women. More and more evidence of this fear, dread, and loathing is being unearthed by feminist scholars every day, revealing a universal prejudice against women that, in all major cultures of recorded patriarchal history, has permeated the thought of seemingly rational and civilized "great men." A quasi-infinite catalog could be compiled of quotes from the male leaders of civilization revealing this universal dread, expressed sometimes as loathing, sometimes ridicule, sometimes patronizing contempt.[182]

An unflattering mind-set toward women was ironically condoned in accounts of religious history. The scriptures of every religion, written long ago by men, reflect this attitude. Strict observance of these scriptures forced women into positions of subservience to men. All the major religions promote a systemic belief in the inferiority of women, placing them on the same level as slaves and children.[183] Nonetheless religious authorities like to argue that their scriptures and laws are sacred and therefore immune to change. There can be little doubt the myth of women's inferiority has been, at least to a certain extent, endorsed and perpetuated by religious beliefs.

When traditions are changed so that women are treated as equals to men, society itself will be transformed. When women are reinstated in the image of God on earth, men will no longer have the lone sovereignty in heaven. By challenging the authority of males on earth, feminists make effective onslaughts on male authority in heaven. The women's movement is destined to spread religious revolution in all levels of popular culture. Vast amounts of human energy will be liberated once millions of men and women are freed from their psychological prisons.[184]

The fact of women's low caste status has been – and is – disguised. Sexual caste is hidden by the fact that women have various forms of status as a consequence of ideologies, relationships to men, and sex role segregation.[185] Whether the situation is trivialized, justified, or ignored, the status of women continues to be below that of men, century after century. Even more insidious is that the history of antifeminism in the Judeo-Christian heritage is defined as being in accord with the divine plan. The entire conceptual system of theology, developed under the conditions of patriarchy, has been the product of males and tends to serve the interests of a sexist society. Christian theology widely asserted that women were inferior, weak, depraved, and vicious.[186]

The biblical story of the fall attempts to explain the confusion of human beings trying to make sense out of the human condition. Women's role as scapegoats has been fostered by Christianity. The fall of man should rightly be called the fall of woman because once more the second sex is blamed for all the troubles in the world. Women, encouraged to imitate the sacrificial love of Jesus, willingly accept the victim's role and remain essentially identified with Eve and evil.[187] As long as the myth of the feminine evil is allowed to dominate human consciousness and social arrangements, it provides the settings for women's victimization by both men and women. The message that it unintentionally conveys is that in patriarchy, with the aid of religion, women have been the primordial scapegoats.[188]

Identification of women with evil has been dysfunctional for both genders. Overcoming sex stereotyping that dichotomizes and hierarchizes all of us is the first step toward liberation. The work of unveiling and actively repudiating this myth of feminine evil requires a shared redemptive action by women. Women have to stop denying the sexism that lies at the root of Jewish and Christian traditions. That is, it will demand a collective effort of all women's energies to repudiate the structures and ideologies of patriarchy. Active, positive, and independent thinking is most effective, as it refuses tokenism or absorption into existing male modalities.

20

Balancing Masculinity and Femininity

Symbols, metaphors and archetypes have influenced culture more than we dare to admit. Yet, women who have analyzed patriarchy know that the image of a white, male God undergirds the whole economic and social system. The picture of a white man in the sky influences the position of every person under that sky. Images of God dictate who will feel worthy in society and who will feel inferior, who will be respected and who will be despised, who will get easy access to the material goods of culture and who will have to fight for those same goods.[189]

When vast numbers of women and men come to realize their innate divine value, social reform and laws like the Equal Rights Amendment will have no trouble passing. Women should not be discriminated against, let alone exploited. The same men that are abusing God's daughters should be protecting and securing their livelihood. Instead of using scriptures to justify women's subordinate place, it should become the reason to fairly balance men's and women's lives in all aspects of the social order. Ironically, men suffer more than women both internally and externally when women are mistreated or oppressed. Suicide rates are higher in men than in women, with males three to four times more likely to kill themselves than females.[190]

Balance requires developing the feminine side. For reasons of survival, liberation, business, and technology, most people have been able to develop their masculine side to a greater extent than the feminine. It may be that it is just easier to learn the lessons of the masculine side, but the result is that, as a species, we are left with a serious masculine/feminine imbalance. And it is a dangerous imbalance because it is a formula for destruction and hurting people. It is time to recognize that the feminine side has value, and that its value lies in knowing and doing what is good for people. It is time to recognize that it is good for people to give and help each other, because that creates less turmoil in the world. It is time to recognize that at this moment in our evolution, most people are here to learn to develop the feminine side, because that is what will give us balance.[191]

Acquiring a sense of balance - of the equality of opposites - is what is needed to save our societies and the earth.[192] Most people cannot accept or understand themselves as being androgynous, a blend of an equal inheritance from our mother and father. Each human cell has forty six chromosomes, half from the father and half from the mother. Once everyone understands their basic makeup, both externally and internally, a clearer, more balanced vision of ourselves and others is possible. Who decided that knowing what you feel or nurturing others is feminine? And why is being potent and in charge considered to be masculine? In reality, these are human qualities, and neither sex has a corner on them.

Unless we find the Goddess within ourselves we will never find Her without. She is both internal and external; as solid as a rock, as changeable as our own internal image of Her. She is manifest within each of us; we are already one with the Goddess - She has been with us since the beginning. So fulfillment becomes not a matter of self-indulgence but of self-awareness. For women, the Goddess is the symbol of the inmost self, and the beneficent, nurturing, liberating power within woman. For a man, the Goddess, as well as the universal life force, is his own, hidden, female self. As he becomes more whole and becomes aware of his own "female" qualities, he too learns to find Her within.[193]

When we look at the development of our species as a whole, technological development could be compared to the masculine side, while spiritual development could be compared to the feminine side. And just as balance is necessary for an individual, it is equally important for us as a species to maintain a balance between our technological and spiritual development. At the present time, the masculine or technological side is too strong compared to the feminine or spiritual side. This is a dangerous position to be in because we have technology that is capable of great destruction. The situation has resulted in an imbalance that occurs from having too much technology for our level of spiritual evolution. To correct this imbalance, it is necessary to develop the feminine side and bring it into closer balance with the masculine side. This will allow us to use our technology without misusing it, not only in areas of conflict or war, but also in areas of caring for our planet in a way that is good for her, and consequently good for us.

Whether male or female, we each have a masculine and feminine side. Everything in the spiritual and physical world dances in a rhythmic flow of male and female energy. Wholeness requires the balancing of our masculine and feminine sides. Our feminine side is nurturing, creative, sensitive, comforting, caring, and patient. She is the healer as well as the teacher. Our masculine side is associated with law, analysis, power, strength, protection, and discipline. When we are out of balance we feel chaotic and lack harmony. We are out of sync with the universe and our energy is scattered. Whether we become uncaring, insensitive, abusive, and aggressive or passive, indecisive, and weak-willed, we become spiritually bankrupt.[194]

There's been a pleasant shift on the planet lately with the increase of feminine energy to balance the masculine energy that has been dominant for so many centuries. As we evolve in consciousness it's necessary to transcend the duality of male and female and honor our spiritual wholeness within. We may have separate bodies – either male or female – but within and beyond we are potent spiritual beings. As we balance our yin and yang energies we come into balance and so does the planet. Women and men who embody their feminine and masculine energy are strong, wise, loving, creative human beings. They appreciate the active yang energy of taking action and setting boundaries when needed, while honoring the nurturing yin energy of stillness and gentleness.[195]

Over many lifetimes each male and female counterpart has been trying to bring his or her masculine and feminine energies into balance. This doesn't mean that a woman has to be half feminine and half masculine. It means that she needs to fully develop her feminine characteristics, while at the same time allowing her masculine side to grow and mature as well. The same idea holds true for a man. When the two twin halves have balanced their masculine and feminine sides and have reached a strong sense of self and spiritual maturity, they are ready for lasting reunion. Thousands of years ago the female energy was the dominant form on this planet; Approximately two thousand years ago it reversed and man's innate fear of woman caused the female energy to be suppressed. Today the feminine energy is rising once again. And its influence is driving the spiritual transformation of our planet and all its inhabitants.[196]

The glory, wisdom, mercy and justice, majesty, intuition, and understanding of God are feminine. These feminine forces are integral to both God and creation. Without the feminine, nothing would be as it is. Thus, God's feminine power is naturally part of everything, inseparable, essential, and universal. That the spirit through whom humans communicate with, connect to, and interact with God is feminine shows the essential power of feminine energy. It also shows that God can relate to humans in varying forms, and that a Feminine Divine force is just as able to communicate with all people as is a Masculine Divine force. From this it may be concluded that human females are just as able to communicate, create, judge, glorify, understand, rule, and exist as men.[197]

Conclusion

As mankind is now re-entering the age of the Mother, Her return will give rebirth and bring about a new spring of re-emerging women cultures. This is not something to hide or be embarrassed about. The whole world needs to know about our Mother and Father God.[198] Solutions can be found when there is a balance of femininity and masculinity. Appreciating that both Mother God and Father God have equally done their fair share in carrying human history is fundamental. It may take some time and diligence, but sooner or later the next generation will be able to better understand the value of the feminine and masculine aspects of God's nature. As Mother God cares for all Her children, we will learn how to care for Her. It is not only sacred but absolutely necessary to have a real, honest give-and-take relationship with our Heavenly Mother, along with our Heavenly Father. Now is the time to break the conspiracy of silence about the feminine side of God.

All people on earth can play a pioneering role in a great transformational process that is unfolding. We are talking about deep changes in our religious subconscious, which has been formed in part by many thousands of years of patriarchal dominance in language.[199] A revived contemporary consciousness of the once-widespread veneration of the female deity as the loving Creatress of the Universe can revive life and civilizations everywhere. The fate of humanity and the earth is connected to how well we receive Her. In reclaiming the Goddess, we can redress the imbalance between the human species and our natural environment, between men and women, with the possibility of living in harmony and justice with all things.[200] Paradoxically, humanity can find out more solutions to who they really are by exploring the ancient past.

Times are changing for women. Now is the time of feminine awakening when the divine birthright of both men and women is reclaimed. After forgiving history and dissolving old constructs of male/female inequalities, the way will be open for a gender-balanced society. The truth is that for the last few millennia, virtually everything we've come to accept as normal has been designed by and for masculine consciousness. By identifying the feminine within all of us, and connecting with the Divine Mother, a new multidimensional, attuned, and embodied way of life will be achievable. This new collective unconsciousness of feminine equality and value will permeate people's lifestyles and give rise to a peaceful civilization quite naturally.

The yearning for a maternal power is strong in modern time. The image of the Goddess has attained new value and attention in recent years – hence the growth of new religious movements that see the vision of the Goddess as their central inspiration.[201] Women have come a long way from the time they were treated as servants or chattel. Over the past thirty years, Goddess feminists have developed practices and understandings that assist women in self-empowerment and self-recovery. Women in the Goddess religion movement describe practices that lead to an experience of cooperation with and faithfulness to an inwardly experienced presence of the divine image in feminine terms as Goddess. The eventual propagation of these new gender-balanced ideas will secure actual changes – even though many are still strongly resisted. Mother and Father God cannot sustain any system, organization, government or religion that does not reflect the original blueprint of gender-balance.

Our sense of balance in all realms of living may cause us to rethink why all the imbalances exist in the world today. There is so much suffering and so much left undone because we cannot bring equality on the earth. To see ourselves as balanced, we must understand balance at our beginnings – the male and female that goes back to the foundation of creation. Leaving femininity out of the image of God has been the source of most of the suffering experienced by both men and women. We are all affected by the lost of the motherly aspect of our Creator. This must be corrected, for the emancipation of the entire society.

We may recognize from scriptures that the Godhead has the attributes of both Father and Mother. Even religions that restrict the vision of God to a patriarchal image only, describe God's love in terms that can be said to encompass both fatherly love (Creator, Teacher, Guide, and Savior) and motherly love (Nurturer, Fount of Compassion, and Sustainer). Yet religious systems have been unable to help us have a direct, complete relationship with the Divine Mother because they could not clearly show the way for a direct birthing of the divine child within us. Inside ourselves is an inherent masculine and feminine duality that connects us to the both sides of the Godhead naturally.

The symbolism of the Goddess has taken on an electrifying power for modern women. The rediscovery of ancient matrifocal civilizations has given women a deep sense of pride in women's ability to create and sustain culture. It has exposed the falsehoods of patriarchal history and given women a role model of female strength and authority. As women constitute at least half of the population, future prosperity for all countries would be ensured if their aptitude and talents were given equal opportunity. Additionally, when men and women share tasks working side by side, the result would produce a truly egalitarian society. Humankind will benefit in more ways than one from the kinder and gentler gender-balanced divinity. Managing the use of pronouns in relating to God would be a good start as God is not just He but also She. Speaking, writing, and reading about God should be in the context of Heavenly Father, Heavenly Mother or both. The Divine King has ruled for thousands of years with the words, "Thou shall not," while the Divine Queen may lead with the words, "You may, but be careful."

God is the male/female parent of all mankind. Until the Divine Mother is welcome back into the hearts of humanity, healing of the planet will not take place. When there is an understanding of the divine feminine nature of God, the world will be transformed into the living image of love and justice. Through the balancing of the masculine and feminine nature of God, a new age of true unity, equality, and richness can come. The spiritual revolution that is trying to be born will not be born until Mother God returns. Through the sacred gender-balance of Father and Mother God in all aspects of society, a genuine "peaceful" revolution will occur. In order to achieve peace on earth, we either become again children of Mother God like our ancient ancestors, or we remain products of the current disorder. A genuine understanding of God's femininity would bring about a complete physical and spiritual bonding together of all life on earth.

We need a new, global spirituality, an organic spirituality that belongs innately to all of us, as the children of the earth. For children, it is very natural to make a relationship with their parents. Many people feel like orphans because they haven't experienced the parental love of Mother God. Once someone is confident in this relationship their outlook on life will transform into a genuine spirituality that utterly refutes the moralistic, manipulative, and mechanistic religions that seek to control and oppress us by successfully dividing us. We need a spirituality that acknowledges our earthly roots as evolutionary and sexual beings, just as we need an ontology that acknowledges earth as a conscious and spiritual being. We should realign ourselves to return to the beginning, to love life, to be aware that we are all living inside the body of God.[202]

Today, women and men in a variety of settings are questioning our exclusive reliance on male metaphors for God. In prayer and study they are rediscovering female imagery for God long hidden in scriptures and traditions. Feminist artists, poets, composers, and theologians are fashioning new images and idioms for God out of women's embodied experience. Language about God is expanding, even to the point of addressing divine mystery as "She." The theological case for such language and its development is of the highest religious significance. Given the ingrained negative assessment of women's humanity under patriarchy, women's experience of themselves in this way is a powerful event, the coming into maturity of suppressed selves. In a religious sense, it is the experience of conversion of heart and mind.

To awaken the Mother's sacred heart in us is to awaken a passion to serve, honor and protect all of nature and all living things. The human race will not be honoring the Mother until every starving person is fed, every homeless person is housed, every sick and poor person has free access to medicine, every woman is free from all kinds of oppression, and every human being is free to experience and express love. The force of the Mother is a revolutionary force of love that works incessantly to break down all barriers and separations in the name of love and hungers to see this world become the stable paradise it already is in her mind of truth.[203]

One has to wonder how the masculine position alone stayed as the central belief of culture and history. As a result of the increasing problems in the world, the age of masculinity is now drawing to a close. What we need now, and what the Divine Mother offers us, is a vision of the holy splendor of the body-spirit and of nature. The revolution of the sacred feminine can only happen when we empower ourselves by establishing a relationship with the Divine Mother. Mother God is offering us union with Her, if only we can open ourselves to Her essential divine nature and live it at every moment. Direct contact with the Divine Mother is the way the great spiritual transformation will occur.[204]

This is the era of women. In the Eastern philosophy book called *The Book of Changes* it is written, "The 5000 years of Yang period is finished. Now the 5000 years of Yin will start." In the family, it is the mother's role to correct and put things back where they were when things go wrong. Once the culture shock of Mother God has worn off, everyone will gradually become accustomed to a more balanced image of God. The invisible Mother God will become "visible" and God will no longer be like a single parent. That humankind has forgotten and rejected Mother God has been truly regrettable but it is only fair to say that Father God's situation has been equally miserable as He has been witnessing this sad state of affairs in solitude.

Epilogue: The Heart of Heavenly Mother

Unfortunately, the world has many problems today, including war, poverty, crime, pollution, disease, over-population, economic downturns, and natural disasters. As a result, life can be uncertain, stressful, and sometimes overwhelming. Every day there are casualties, whether psychological or physical, that causes people to suffer grievously. What most people do not know is that Mother God shares their suffering as a parent. Terror, disappointment, destruction, and sadness can change into forgiveness, hope, and love once Mother God has the resources to manage and deal with these problems. Mother God Herself has been unsuccessful in bringing peace to the hopes of beating hearts, to families, and to nations. This endless cycle has been going on for thousands of years, causing our Heavenly Parent tremendous frustration.

Most people are unaware that God lives in and through each one of us. It is incredible that Mother God feels the pain of victims of suffering and allows Herself to experience it in order to provide comfort for each of Her children. Yet little or no appreciation, recognition, or credit is given to Mother God for Her centuries of quiet effort. In fact, there is very little understanding of what part She plays and what Her contributions have been in the healing of humankind. She always wants to be an integral part of each family and of the history of the world.

Mother God still doesn't know how to convince the majority of humanity to open their hearts, trust in Her, believe in Her, and be loved by Her. Still, there are some who know the heart of Mother God. They know Her grief, Her heartache, and they spend time comforting Her, hearing Her, and holding her hand. They are the true sons and daughters who know their Parent's grief. More important, they want to end it by bringing success and happiness for all so that we can get beyond the grief. Understanding God as a being of original masculinity and femininity would be the first step in solving many of the problems in the world to-day. The next step would be a cohesive, united response to Her loving suggestions on how to improve the current situation.

Instead of ignoring or disregarding Mother God, religions should transcend and unite with other religions and by embracing Her as a parent. The ignorance about the feminine side of the Godhead has to end. Once the world understands that there is a Mother God along with a Father God, a gender-balanced society can begin to appear. Unity, equity and peace will happen automatically while war, crime and poverty will be things of the distant past. Now is the time to reap the benefits of true love by getting to know our heavenly parents and subsequently our own divine nature. At that moment, we will all know that we are inside Mother God and that Mother God is inside us.

Related Websites

1. http://www.sacredwind.com/divinemother.php

2. http://en.wikipedia.org/wiki/Heavenly_Mother

3. http://www.mother-god.com/

4. https://en.wikipedia.org/wiki/Goddess

5. http://en.wikipedia.org/wiki/Mother_goddess

6. http://en.wikipedia.org/wiki/Matriarchal_religion

7. http://www.tparents.org/Library/Unification/Publications/ JUS-7-2006/JUS-7-2006-5.htm

8. http://www.godweb.org/motherhoodofgod.htm

9. http://www.themystica.org/mystica/articles/g/goddess_3_ the_mother.html

10. http://www.thesongofgod.com/topical_guide/heavenly_ mother.html

11. http://www.sophiastemple.com/the-divine-feminine/

12. http://www.northernway.org/sophia.html

13. http://sophiafoundation.org/

14. http://mother.watv.org/eng/index.asp

15. http://www.womanthouartgod.com/main.php

16. http://en.wikipedia.org/wiki/Goddess_movement

17. http://www.goddessariadne.org/whywomenneedthegoddess.htm

18. http://eternalfeminine.wikispaces.com/Dea+-+the+Essential+Image+of+Divinity

19. http://en.wikipedia.org/wiki/Wicca

20. https://en.wikipedia.org/wiki/Marian_apparition

21. http://en.wikipedia.org/wiki/Heavenly_Mother_%28Mormonism%29

22. http://www.net-burst.net/god/mother.htm#top

23. http://www.lovesedona.com/02.htm

24. http://ideas.time.com/2013/05/11/why-god-is-a-mother-too/

25. http://dmpatrium.org/2013/05/10/god-the-mother-series-pt-1-gods-image/

26. http://www.wheeloftheyear.com/reference/hildegard.htm

27. http://www.universalspiritualview.com/divine_feminine_energy.htm

28. http://www.jeshua.net/healing/healing5.htm

29. http://www.indigosun.com/old_files/JULY99/Laurel.htm

30. http://ginigrey.com/spiritualtransformers/balance-your-divine-feminine-and-masculine-energy/

31. http://ruthieogrant.org/articles/Balancing%20Our%20Masculine%20and%20Feminine%20Energies.htm

32. http://en.wikipedia.org/wiki/Anima_and_animus

33. http://www.csmonitor.com/1988/0906/mrc776.html

34. http://www.ascendedmasterindex.com/gods.htm

35. http://www.summitlighthouse.org/Reading-Room/inner-perspectives/6God-As-Mother.html

36. http://www.northernway.org/school/omm.shtml

37. http://www.huffingtonpost.com/pauline-muchina/gender-inequality-what-is-gods-agenda_b_3390419.html

38. http://www2.kenyon.edu/Depts/Religion/Projects/Reln91/Gender/godlang&femchristology.htm

39. http://deoxy.org/gaia/goddess.htm

40. http://www.angelfire.com/wa3/ladyaurora/goddess.htm

41. http://www.wordiq.com/definition/Goddess

42. http://www.sccs.swarthmore.edu/users/99/maya/sarah.html

43. http://www.interfaithmary.net/pages/mary_goddess.html

44. http://www.ancient-wisdom.co.uk/earthmother.htm

45. http://www.goddess.ws/

46. http://landofgoddesses.wordpress.com/2012/03/11/demeter-ceres/

47. http://www.fact-index.com/g/go/goddess.html

48. http://www.shira.net/egypt-goddess.htm

49. http://www.themystica.com/mystica/articles/g/goddess_1_intro_and_history.html

50. http://pinterest.com/mothergaiaelle/god-goddess-holy-symbols/

51. http://www.rahoorkhuit.net/goddess/herstory/ancient_mother.html

52. http://www.religionfacts.com/hinduism/deities/goddesses.htm

53. http://www.truthbeknown.com/mary.html

54. http://mysticgoddess.org/goddesses.htm

55. http://www.egreenway.com/meditation/goddess1.htm

56. http://www.northernway.org/goddess.html

57. http://www.ignatiusinsight.com/features2005/mhauke_maryfem_july05.asp

58. http://atlantisonline.smfforfree2.com/index.php?topic=1310.0

59. http://www.leaderu.com/orgs/probe/docs/goddess.html

60. http://www.factmonster.com/ipka/A0768471.html

61. http://www.religioustolerance.org/goddess.htm

62. http://www.enlightenedbeings.com/healing-goddess.html

63. http://jeanbakula.hubpages.com/hub/_Sophia-Greek-Goddess-of-Spiritual-Wisdom

64. https://en.wikipedia.org/wiki/Mazu_%28goddess%29

65. http://www.20000-names.com/goddess_names.htm

66. http://www.goddess.org/

67. http://goddesstimeline.com/?page_id=16

68. http://www.equalrightsamendment.org/

69. http://en.wikipedia.org/wiki/History_of_feminism

70. http://en.wikipedia.org/wiki/First-wave_feminism

71. http://en.wikipedia.org/wiki/Second-wave_feminism

72. http://www.telshemesh.org/shekhinah/

73. http://www2.kenyon.edu/Depts/Religion/Projects/Reln91/Gender/MYSTICISM.htm

74. http://centerforchristconsciousness.wordpress.com/category/messages-from-mother-nebadonia/

75. http://en.wikipedia.org/wiki/Misogyny

76. http://en.wikipedia.org/wiki/Mother_of_God

77. http://en.wikipedia.org/wiki/Earth_Goddess

78. http://en.wikipedia.org/wiki/Mother_Nature

79. http://emissaries.org/2011/05/09/the-divine-feminine/

80. http://trceandthewell.org/Tree_and_the_Well/Sacred_Feminine.html

81. http://www.mothergod.info

Bibliography

Aurobindo, Sri, *The Mother,* Lotus Press, Twin Lakes, WI, 1995

Briffault, Robert, *The Mothers,* Atheneum, New York, 1977

Brown, Sylvia, *God, Creation and Tools for Life,* Hay House, Carlsbadt, CA, 2000

Brown, Sylvia, *Mother God,* Hay House, Carlsbadt, CA, 2004

Bulkeley, Tim, *Not Only A Father,* Archer Press, New Zealand, 2011

Cambell, Joseph, *The Power of Myth,* First Anchor Books, NY, 1998

Cambell, Joseph, *In All Her Names: Explorations of the Feminine in Divinity,* Harper, CA, 1991

Charlton, Hilda, *Divine Mother Speaks,* Golden Quest, Woodstock, NY, 1993

Christ, Carol B., *Rebirth of the Goddess,* Routledge, New York, 1997

Carson, Anne, *Feminist Spirituality and the Feminine Divine*, Crossing Press, NY, 1986

Crandall, Barbara, *Gender and Religion,* Continuum Int'l Publishing Group, NY, 2012

Daly, Mary, *Beyond God the Father,* Beacon Press, Boston, MA, 1973

Eisler, Riane, *The Chalice and the Blade,* Harper & Row, S.F., CA, 1987

Engelsman, Joan C., *The Feminine Dimension of the Divine,* Chiron Pub.,Wilmette, IL, 1994

Gadon, Elinor W., *The Once and Future Goddess*, Harper & Row Publishers, S.F., CA, 1989

Goldenberg, Naomi, *Changing of the Gods,* Beacon Press, Boston, MA, 1979

Gumbutas, Marija, *The Living Goddesses*, Univ. of Calif. Press, Berkeley, CA, 1999

Harvey, Andrew & Baring, Anne, *The Divine Feminine*, Conari Press, Berkeley, CA, 1996

Harvey, Andrew, *The Return of the Mother*, Frog Ltd., Berkeley, CA, 1995

Hermitage, *Sophia, The Holy Spirit*, La Ermita, Macon, GA. 2010

James, E.O., *The Cult of the Mother Goddess*, Barnes & Noble, NY, 1994

Jennings, Victoria, *God as Mother*, Inner Search Books, CA, 2002

Kassian, Mary, *The Feminist Mistake,* Crossway Books, Wheaton, IL, 2005

Kunzli, Josef, *The Messages of the Lady of All Nations*, Queenship Publishing, CA, 1996

Markale, Jean, *The Great Goddess*. Inner Traditions, Rochester, VT, 1997

Matthews, Caitlin, *Sophia, Goddess of Wisdom, Bride of God*, Quest Books, IL. 2001

Mollenkott, Virginia Ramey, *The Divine Feminine*, Crossroads Publishing, NY, 1989

Moon, Sun Myung, *Exposition of the Divine Principle*, HSA-UWC Publications, NY, 1996

Motz, Lotte, *The Faces of the Goddess*, Oxford University Press, NY, 1997

Muses, Charles & Cambell, Joseph, *In All Her Names*, Harper, S.F., CA, 1991

Neumann, Erich, *The Great Mother*, Princeton University Press, Princeton, NJ, 1955

Newman, Barbara, *Sister of Wisdom*, Univ. of CA. Press, Berkeley, CA, 1987

Nicholson, Shirley, *The Goddess Re-Awakening*, Theosophical Publishing House, IL, 1989

Ochs, Carol, *Behind the Sex of God*, Beacon Press, Boston, MA, 1977

Olson, Carl, *The Book of Goddess, Past & Present*, Waveland Press, IL, 1983

Pagels, Elaine, *The Gnostic Gospels*, Vintage Books, NY, 1979

Pappalardo, Ron, *Reconciled by the Light, Book II,* CPSIA, NC, 2013

Pirani, Alix, *The Absent Mother,* Mandala, London, 1991

Powell, Robert, *The Sophia Teaching,* Lindisfarne Books, MA, 2001

Pratt M.D., Marilyn J., *God's Femininity Recognized,* Golden Puer Publishing, CA, 1980

Raphael, Melissa, *Introducing Thealogy,* The Pilgrim Press, Cleveland, OH, 2000

Stadelhofer, Shirley, *New Truth in the Last Days,* iUniverse Inc. NY, 2006

Starhawk, *The Spiral Dance,* Harper, San Francisco, CA, 1979

Sjoo, Monica and Mor, Barbara. *The Great Cosmic Mother,* Harper & Row, NY, 1987

Smith, Paul R., *Is It Okay to Call God "Mother"?* Henderson Publishers, Peabody, MA, 1993

Stone, Merlin, *When God Was a Woman,* Harcourt Brace & Co., Orlando, FL, 1976

Vaughn-Lee, Lee, *The Return of the Feminine & the World Soul,* Golden Sufi, CA, 2009

Whitmont, Edward C., *Return of the Goddess,* Crossroads Publishing, NY, 1982

Endnotes

Introduction

1   Merlin Stone, *When God Was a Woman*, (Harcourt Brace & Co, FL, 1976) 9

2   Sylvia Brown, *Mother God*, (Hay House, Carlsbad, CA, 2004) 43

3   Joseph Cambell, Charles Muse, *In All Her Names,* (Harper, S.F., CA, 1991) 5

4   E.O. James, *The Cult of the Mother Goddess*, (Barnes & Noble, NY, 1994) 11

5   Elinor W. Gadon, *The Once and Future Goddess*, (Harper & Row, S.F., CA, 1989) xiii

6   Carol Ochs, *Behind the Sex of God,* (Beacon Press, Boston, MA, 1977) 70

7   Victoria Jennings, *God as Mother*, (Inner Search Books, 2002) 126

8   Monica Sjoo, *The Great Cosmic Mother*, (Harper, San Francisco, CA, 1987) 12

9   Monica Sjoo, *The Great Cosmic Mother*, (Harper, San Francisco, CA, 1987) 30

10   Paul R. Smith, *Is It Okay to Call God "Mother"*, (Henrickson Publishers, Peabody, MA, 1993) 162

11   Sylvia Brown, *Mother God*, (Hay House, CA, 2004) 106

1
The Great Goddess:
Divine Feminine from the Past to the Present

12   Jean Markale, *The Great Goddess*, (Inner Traditions, Rochester, VT, 1997) 62

13   Jean Markale, *The Great Goddess*, (Inner Traditions, Rochester, VT, 1997) 103

14   Jean Markale, *The Great Goddess*, (Inner Traditions, Rochester, VT, 1997) 116

15   Jean Markale, *The Great Goddess*, (Inner Traditions, Rochester, VT, 1997) 176

16   Jean Markale, *The Great Goddess*, (Inner Traditions, Rochester, VT, 1997) 206

17   Jean Markale, *The Great Goddess*, (Inner Traditions, Rochester, VT, 1997) 134

18 Jean Markale, *The Great Goddess*, (Inner Traditions, Rochester, VT, 1997) 148

19 Jean Markale, *The Great Goddess*, (Inner Traditions, Rochester, VT, 1997) 216

20 Jean Markale, *The Great Goddess*, (Inner Traditions, Rochester, VT, 1997) 219

21 Jean Markale, *The Great Goddess*, (Inner Traditions, Rochester, VT, 1997) 125

22 Jean Markale, *The Great Goddess*, (Inner Traditions, Rochester, VT, 1997) 126

2
The Return of the Mother

23 Andrew Harvey, *The Return of the Mother*, (Frog Ltd, Berkeley, CA, 1995) 13

24 Andrew Harvey, *The Return of the Mother*, (Frog Ltd, Berkeley, CA, 1995) 11

25 Andrew Harvey, *The Return of the Mother*, (Frog Ltd, Berkeley, CA, 1995) 12

26 Andrew Harvey, *The Return of the Mother*, (Frog Ltd, Berkeley, CA, 1995) 132

27 Andrew Harvey, *The Return of the Mother*, (Frog Ltd, Berkeley, CA, 1995) 74

28 Andrew Harvey, *The Return of the Mother*, (Frog Ltd, Berkeley, CA, 1995) 143

29 Andrew Harvey, *The Return of the Mother*, (Frog Ltd, Berkeley, CA, 1995) 295

30 Andrew Harvey, *The Return of the Mother*, (Frog Ltd, Berkeley, CA, 1995) 39

31 Andrew Harvey, *The Return of the Mother*, (Frog Ltd, Berkeley, CA, 1995) 112

32 Andrew Harvey, *The Return of the Mother*, (Frog Ltd, Berkeley, CA, 1995) 35

3
The Sophia Teachings

33 Robert Powell, *The Sophia Teachings,* (Lindisfarne Books, MA, 2001) 2

34 Robert Powell, *The Sophia Teachings,* (Lindisfarne Books, MA, 2001) 30

35 Robert Powell, *The Sophia Teachings,* (Lindisfarne Books, MA, 2001) 141

36 La Ermita, *Sophia, The Holy Spirit*, (The Hermitage, Macon, GA.,2010) 5

37 Robert Powell, *The Sophia Teachings,* (Lindisfarne Books, MA, 2001) 43

38 Robert Powell, *The Sophia Teachings,* (Lindisfarne Books, MA, 2001) 52

39 Robert Powell, *The Sophia Teachings,* (Lindisfarne Books, MA, 2001) 15

40   Robert Powell, *The Sophia Teachings,* (Lindisfarne Books, MA, 2001) 14

41   Robert Powell, *The Sophia Teachings,* (Lindisfarne Books, MA, 2001) 132

42   Robert Powell, *The Sophia Teachings,* (Lindisfarne Books, MA, 2001) 21-22

4
The Return of the Feminine

43   Llewellyn Vaugh-Lee, *The Return of the Feminine and the World Soul,* (The Golden Sufi Center, CA, 2009) 32-33

44   Llewellyn Vaugh-Lee, *The Return of the Feminine and the World Soul,* (The Golden Sufi Center, CA, 2009) 4

45   Llewellyn Vaugh-Lee, *The Return of the Feminine and the World Soul,* (The Golden Sufi Center, CA, 2009) 14

46   Llewellyn Vaugh-Lee, *The Return of the Feminine and the World Soul,* (The Golden Sufi Center, CA, 2009) 7

47   Llewellyn Vaugh-Lee, *The Return of the Feminine and the World Soul,* (The Golden Sufi Center, CA, 2009) 11

48   Llewellyn Vaugh-Lee, *The Return of the Feminine and the World Soul,* (The Golden Sufi Center, CA, 2009) 114

49   Llewellyn Vaugh-Lee, *The Return of the Feminine and the World Soul,* (The Golden Sufi Center, CA, 2009) 12

50   Llewellyn Vaugh-Lee, *The Return of the Feminine and the World Soul,* (The Golden Sufi Center, CA, 2009) 59

5
The Rebirth of the Goddess

51   Carol B. Christ, *Rebirth of the Goddess*, (Routledge, NY, 1997) 44

52   Robert Briffault, *The Mothers*, (Atheneum, NY, 2007) 363-64

53   Robert Briffault, *The Mothers*, (Atheneum, NY, 2007) 375

54   Robert Briffault, *The Mothers*, (Atheneum, NY, 2007) 377

55   Robert Briffault, *The Mothers*, (Atheneum, NY, 2007) 375

56   Carol B. Christ, *Rebirth of the Goddess*, (Routledge, NY, 1997) 30

6
The Goddess Religion

57   Carol B. Christ, *Rebirth of the Goddess*, (Routledge, NY, 1997) 105

58   Carol B. Christ, *Rebirth of the Goddess*, (Routledge, NY, 1997) 106

59   Carol B. Christ, *Rebirth of the Goddess*, (Routledge, NY, 1997) 106

60   Carol B. Christ, *Rebirth of the Goddess*, (Routledge, NY, 1997) 107

61   Carol B. Christ, *Rebirth of the Goddess*, (Routledge, NY, 1997) 167

62   Carol B. Christ, *Rebirth of the Goddess*, (Routledge, NY, 1997) 78

63   Carol B. Christ, *Rebirth of the Goddess*, (Routledge, NY, 1997) 69

7
Gnostic Ideas

64   Elaine Pagels, *The Gnostic Gospels,* (Vintage Books, NY, 1979) 37

65   Elaine Pagels, *The Gnostic Gospels,* (Vintage Books, NY, 1979) 52

8
Myth and Reality

66   Edward C. Whitmont, *Return of the Goddess*,(Crossroads Publishing, NY, 1982) 40

67   Edward C. Whitmont, *Return of the Goddess*,(Crossroads Publishing, NY, 1982) viii

68   Starhawk, *The Spiral Dance, (*Harper, San Francisco, CA, 1979) 32

69   Edward C. Whitmont, *Return of the Goddess*,(Crossroads Publishing, NY, 1982) 78

70   Edward C. Whitmont, *Return of the Goddess*,(Crossroads Publishing, NY, 1982) 13

9
Mother God

71   Barbara Newman, *Sister of Wisdom*, (Univ. of Calif. Press, Berkeley, CA, 1987) 47

72   Sylvia Brown, *God, Creation and Tools for Life,* (Hay House, CA, 2000) 54

73   Sylvia Brown, *God, Creation and Tools for Life,* (Hay House, CA, 2000) 11

74   Sylvia Brown, *God, Creation and Tools for Life,* (Hay House, CA, 2000) 15

75   Sylvia Brown, *God, Creation and Tools for Life,* (Hay House, CA, 2000) 43

10
The Divine Feminine

76 Virginia Ramey Mollenkott, *The Divine Feminine*, (Crossroads, NY, 1989) 27

77 Virginia Ramey Mollenkott, *The Divine Feminine*, (Crossroads, NY, 1989) 29

78 Virginia Ramey Mollenkott, *The Divine Feminine*, (Crossroads, NY, 1989) 9

79 Virginia Ramey Mollenkott, *The Divine Feminine*, (Crossroads, NY, 1989) 10

80 Virginia Ramey Mollenkott, *The Divine Feminine*, (Crossroads, NY, 1989) 65

81 Virginia Ramey Mollenkott, *The Divine Feminine*, (Crossroads, NY, 1989) 14

82 Virginia Ramey Mollenkott, *The Divine Feminine*, (Crossroads, NY, 1989) 16

83 Virginia Ramey Mollenkott, *The Divine Feminine*, (Crossroads, NY, 1989) 87

84 Virginia Ramey Mollenkott, *The Divine Feminine*, (Crossroads, NY, 1989) 112

85 Andrew Harvey, *The Divine Feminine*, (Conari Press, Berkeley, CA, 1996) 7

86 Andrew Harvey, *The Divine Feminine*, (Conari Press, Berkeley, CA, 1996) 6

11
Thealogy

87   Anne Carson, *Feminist Spirituality and the Feminine Divine,* (Crossing Press, NY, 1986) 5

88   Riane Eisler, *The Chalice and the Blade,* (Harper & Row, S.F., CA, 1988) xvi

89   Melissa Raphael, *Introducing Thealogy,* (Pilgrim Press, OH, 2000) 16

90   Melissa Raphael, *Introducing Thealogy,* (Pilgrim Press, OH, 2000) 19

91   Melissa Raphael, *Introducing Thealogy,* (Pilgrim Press, OH, 2000) 15

92   Melissa Raphael, *Introducing Thealogy,* (Pilgrim Press, OH, 2000) 62

93   Melissa Raphael, *Introducing Thealogy,* (Pilgrim Press, OH, 2000) 75

12
The Principle of Creation

94   Sun Myung Moon, *Cheon Seong Gyeong,* (Sunghwa Publishing, Korea, 2006) 1630

95   http://www.newworldencyclopedia.org/entry/ Sun_Myung_Moon

96   Sun Myung Moon, *Expositon of the Divine Principle,* (HSA-UWC, 1996) 19

97   Sun Myung Moon, *Expositon of the Divine Principle, (*HSA-UWC, NY, 1996) 283

98   Glenn Carroll Strait, *Conceptualizing God as Divine Mother and Father*, (2013) 8

99   Carol Ochs, *Behind the Sex of God*, (Beacon Press, Boston, MA, 1977) 110

100 Andrew Wilson, *World Scriptures & the Teachings of Sun Myung Moon, (*UPF Publ., Tarrytown, NY, 2007) 53

101 Sun Myung Moon, *Expositon of the Divine Principle, (*HSA-UWC, NY, 1996) 164

102 Sun Myung Moon, *Cheon Seong Gyeong*, (Sunghwa Publishing, Korea, 2006) 1635

13
Insights on Mother God's Nature

103 Llewellyn Vaugh-Lee, *The Return of the Feminine and the World Soul*, (The Golden Sufi Center, CA, 2009) 6

104 http://www.sacredwind.com/divinemother.php

105 Carol B. Christ, *Rebirth of the Goddess*, (Routledge, NY, 1997) 2

106 http://www.universalspiritualview.com/divine_feminine_energy.htm

107 Sri Aurobindo, *The Mother,* (Lotus Press, Twin Lake, WI, 1995) 40

108 Andrew Harvey, *The Return of the Mother*, (Frog Ltd, Berkeley, CA, 1995) 136

109 Jean Markale, *The Great Goddess*, (Inner Traditions, Rochester, VT, 1997) 70

110 Jean Markale, *The Great Goddess*, (Inner Traditions, Rochester, VT, 1997) 74

111 Barbara Newman, *Sister of Wisdom*, (Univ. of Calif. Press, Berkeley, CA, 1987) 87

112 Sylvia Brown, *God, Creation and Tools for Life,* (Hay House, CA, 2000) 53

113 Sylvia Brown, *God, Creation and Tools for Life,* (Hay House, CA, 2000) 45

114 Andrew Harvey, *The Return of the Mother*, (Frog Ltd, Berkeley, CA, 1995) 118

115 Andrew Harvey, *The Return of the Mother*, (Frog Ltd, Berkeley, CA, 1995) 126

14
When God Was a Woman

116 Merlin Stone, *When God Was a Woman*, (Harcourt Brace & Co, FL, 1976) 15

117 Merlin Stone, *When God Was a Woman*, (Harcourt Brace & Co, FL, 1976) 102

118 Merlin Stone, *When God Was a Woman*, (Harcourt Brace & Co, FL, 1976) 61

119 Merlin Stone, *When God Was a Woman*, (Harcourt Brace & Co, FL, 1976) 68

120 Merlin Stone, *When God Was a Woman*, (Harcourt Brace & Co, FL, 1976) 20

121 Merlin Stone, *When God Was a Woman*, (Harcourt Brace & Co, FL, 1976) 18

122 Merlin Stone, *When God Was a Woman*, (Harcourt Brace & Co, FL, 1976) 52

123 Merlin Stone, *When God Was a Woman*, (Harcourt Brace & Co, FL, 1976) 179

124 Merlin Stone, *When God Was a Woman*, (Harcourt Brace & Co, FL, 1976) 182

125 Merlin Stone, *When God Was a Woman*, (Harcourt Brace & Co, FL, 1976) 163

126 Merlin Stone, *When God Was a Woman*, (Harcourt Brace & Co, FL, 1976) 167

127 Merlin Stone, *When God Was a Woman*, (Harcourt Brace & Co, FL, 1976) 160

128 Merlin Stone, *When God Was a Woman*, (Harcourt Brace & Co, FL. 1976) 217

129 Merlin Stone, *When God Was a Woman*, (Harcourt Brace & Co, FL, 1976) 193

130 Merlin Stone, *When God Was a Woman*, (Harcourt Brace & Co, FL, 1976) 224

131 Merlin Stone, *When God Was a Woman*, (Harcourt Brace & Co, FL, 1976) 238

15
The Goddess Re-Awakening

132   Alix Pirani, *The Absent Mother,* (Mandala, London, 1991) 132

133   Shirley Nicholson, *The Goddess Re-Awakening,* (Theosophical Publishing, IL, 1989) 37

134   Alix Pirani, *The Absent Mother,* (Mandala, London, 1991) 64

135   Shirley Nicholson, *The Goddess Re-Awakening,* (Theosophical Publishing, IL, 1989) 92

136   Alix Pirani, *The Absent Mother,* (Mandala, London, 1991) 92

137   Alix Pirani, *The Absent Mother,* (Mandala, London, 1991) 70

138   Llewellyn Vaugh-Lee, *The Return of the Feminine and the World Soul*, (The Golden Sufi Center, CA, 2009) 49

16
Is It OK to Call God, "Mother"?

139   Paul R. Smith, *Is It Okay to Call God "Mother"*, (Henrickson Publishers, Peabody, MA, 1993) 69

140   Paul R. Smith, *Is It Okay to Call God "Mother"*, (Henrickson Publishers, Peabody, MA, 1993) 87

141   Paul R. Smith, *Is It Okay to Call God "Mother"*, (Henrickson Publishers, Peabody, MA, 1993) 73

142 Paul R. Smith, *Is It Okay to Call God "Mother"*, (Henrickson Publishers, Peabody, MA, 1993) 75

143 Paul R. Smith, *Is It Okay to Call God "Mother"*, (Henrickson Publishers, Peabody, MA, 1993) 160

144 Paul R. Smith, *Is It Okay to Call God "Mother"*, (Henrickson Publishers, Peabody, MA, 1993) 161

145 Paul R. Smith, *Is It Okay to Call God "Mother"*, (Henrickson Publishers, Peabody, MA, 1993) 151

146 Paul R. Smith, *Is It Okay to Call God "Mother"*, (Henrickson Publishers, Peabody, MA, 1993) 198

147 Paul R. Smith, *Is It Okay to Call God "Mother"*, (Henrickson Publishers, Peabody, MA, 1993) 206

148 Paul R. Smith, *Is It Okay to Call God "Mother"*, (Henrickson Publishers, Peabody, MA, 1993) 107

149 Paul R. Smith, *Is It Okay to Call God "Mother"*, (Henrickson Publishers, Peabody, MA, 1993) 162

150 Paul R. Smith, *Is It Okay to Call God "Mother"*, (Henrickson Publishers, Peabody, MA, 1993) 105

151 Paul R. Smith, *Is It Okay to Call God "Mother"*, (Henrickson Publishers, Peabody, MA, 1993) 104

152 Paul R. Smith, *Is It Okay to Call God "Mother"*, (Henrickson Publishers, Peabody, MA, 1993) 147

153 Paul R. Smith, *Is It Okay to Call God "Mother"*, (Henrickson Publishers, Peabody, MA, 1993) 181

154 Paul R. Smith, *Is It Okay to Call God "Mother"*, (Henrickson Publishers, Peabody, MA, 1993) 169

155   Paul R. Smith, *Is It Okay to Call God "Mother"*, (Henrickson Publishers, Peabody, MA, 1993) 164

156   Paul R. Smith, *Is It Okay to Call God "Mother"*, (Henrickson Publishers, Peabody, MA, 1993) 170

157   Paul R. Smith, *Is It Okay to Call God "Mother"*, (Henrickson Publishers, Peabody, MA, 1993) 199

158   Paul R. Smith, *Is It Okay to Call God "Mother"*, (Henrickson Publishers, Peabody, MA, 1993) 193

17
The Feminine Dimension of the Divine

159   Joan Chamberlain Engelsman, *The Feminine Dimension of the Divine*, Chiron, IL, 1994) 11

160   Joan Chamberlain Engelsman, *The Feminine Dimension of the Divine*, Chiron, IL, 1994) 120

161   Alix Pirani, *The Absent Mother*, (Mandala, London, 1991) 106

162   Andrew Harvey, *The Return of the Mother*, (Frog Ltd, Berkeley, CA, 1995) 375

163   Joan Chamberlain Engelsman, *The Feminine Dimension of the Divine*, Chiron, IL, 1994) 132

164   Joan Chamberlain Engelsman, *The Feminine Dimension of the Divine*, Chiron, IL, 1994) 18

18
The Great Cosmic Mother

165 Monica Sjoo, *The Great Cosmic Mother*, (Harper, San Francisco, CA, 1987) 49

166 Monica Sjoo, *The Great Cosmic Mother*, (Harper, San Francisco, CA, 1987) 50

167 Monica Sjoo, *The Great Cosmic Mother*, (Harper, San Francisco, CA, 1987) 90

168 Monica Sjoo, *The Great Cosmic Mother*, (Harper, San Francisco, CA, 1987) 63

169 Monica Sjoo, *The Great Cosmic Mother*, (Harper, San Francisco, CA, 1987) 46

170 Monica Sjoo, *The Great Cosmic Mother*, (Harper, San Francisco, CA, 1987) 213

171 Monica Sjoo, *The Great Cosmic Mother*, (Harper, San Francisco, CA, 1987) 241

172 Monica Sjoo, *The Great Cosmic Mother*, (Harper, San Francisco, CA, 1987) 264

173 Monica Sjoo, *The Great Cosmic Mother*, (Harper, San Francisco, CA, 1987) 410

174 Monica Sjoo, *The Great Cosmic Mother*, (Harper, San Francisco, CA, 1987) 65

175 Monica Sjoo, *The Great Cosmic Mother*, (Harper, San Francisco, CA, 1987) 253

176 Monica Sjoo, *The Great Cosmic Mother*, (Harper, San Francisco, CA, 1987) 365

177 Monica Sjoo, *The Great Cosmic Mother*, (Harper, San Francisco, CA, 1987) 359

178 Monica Sjoo, *The Great Cosmic Mother*, (Harper, San Francisco, CA, 1987) 389

19
The Myth of the Evil Feminine

179 Monica Sjoo, *The Great Cosmic Mother*, (Harper, San Francisco, CA, 1987) 298

180 Barbara Crandall, *Gender and Religion*, (Continuum Int'l Publishing Group, NY, 2012) 201

181 Barbara Crandall, *Gender and Religion*, (Continuum Int'l Publishing Group, NY, 2012) 204

182 Mary Daly, *Beyond God the Father*, (Beacon Press, Boston, 1973) 92

183 Barbara Crandall, *Gender and Religion*, Continuum Inter'l Publishing, NY, 2012) 5

184 Naomi Goldenberg, *Changing of the Gods*, (Beacon Press, Boston, MA, 1979) 36

185 Mary Daly, *Beyond God the Father*, (Beacon Press, Boston, MA, 1973) 2

186 Mary Daly, *Beyond God the Father*, (Beacon Press, Boston, MA, 1973) 95

187 Mary Daly, *Beyond God the Father,* (Beacon Press, Boston, MA, 1973) 77

188 Mary Daly, *Beyond God the Father,* (Beacon Press, Boston, MA, 1973) 47

20
Balancing Masculinity and Femininity

189 Naomi Goldenberg, *Changing of the Gods,* (Beacon Press, Boston, 1979) 126

190 http://en.wikipedia.org/wiki/Suicide

191 http://www.lovesedona.com/02.htm

192 Mayilynn J. Pratt M.D., *God's Femininity Recognized,* (Golden Puer Publishing, CA, 1980) 144

193 Starhawk, *The Spiral Dance,* (Harper, San Francisco, CA, 1979) 111

194 http://www.sacredwind.com/divinemother.php

195 http://ginigrey.com/spiritualtransformers/balance-your-divine-feminine-and-masculine-energy/

196 http://www.fromthestars.com/_printed%20pages/page128p.html

197 http://www2.kenyon.edu/Depts/Religion/Projects/Reln91/Gender/MYSTICISM.htm

Conclusion

198 Paul R. Smith, *Is It Okay to Call God "Mother"*, (Henrickson Publishers, Peabody, MA., 1993) 256

199 Paul R. Smith, *Is It Okay to Call God "Mother"*, (Henrickson Publishers, Peabody, MA, 1993) 218

200 Elinor W. Gadon, *The Once and Future Goddess*, (Harper & Row, S.F., CA, 1989) xv

201 Lotte Motz, *The Faces of the Goddess*, (Oxford Univ. Press, NY, 1997) 23

202 Monica Sjoo, *The Great Cosmic Mother*, (Harper, San Francisco, CA, 1987) 420

203 Andrew Harvey, *The Return of the Mother*, (Frog Ltd, Berkeley, CA, 1995) 446

204 Andrew Harvey, *The Return of the Mother*, (Frog Ltd, Berkeley, CA, 1995) 460

CPSIA information can be obtained at www.ICGtesting.com
Printed in the USA
BVOW02s1339081113

335818BV00007B/78/P